TO, THE WOMAN OF FAITH

TO, THE WOMAN OF FAITH

STACEY RHONWEN MACWAN

Copyright © 2026 by Stacey Rhonwen Macwan

All rights reserved. No part of this book may be reproduced in any manner whatsoever without written permission except in the case of brief quotations embodied in critical articles and reviews.

First Printing, 2026

ISBN: 978-1-7641247-7-5
eISBN: 978-1-7641247-8-2

Unless otherwise stated, **Scripture quotations are taken from** the Holy Bible, New International Version®, NIV®. Copyright © 1973, 1978, 1984, 2011 by Biblica, Inc.® Used by permission of Zondervan. All rights reserved worldwide. www.zondervan.com. The "NIV" and "New International Version" are trademarks registered in the United States Patent and Trademark Office by Biblica, Inc.®

Scriptures marked NKJV are taken from the NEW KING JAMES VERSION (NKJV): Scripture taken from the NEW KING JAMES VERSION®. Copyright© 1982 by Thomas Nelson, Inc. Used by permission. All rights reserved. Scriptures marked ESV are taken from the THE HOLY BIBLE, ENGLISH STANDARD VERSION (ESV): Scriptures taken from THE HOLY BIBLE, ENGLISH STANDARD

Edited and Published by Bekker Media, Australia, www.bekkermedia.com

Cover design by RNBishere

Contents

Dedication   vii
Foreword   ix

Introduction   1
1. Fearfully And Wonderfully Made   3
2. Promises   11
3. Tethered Heart   23
4. Wisdom   37
5. Pursuing God   47
6. Anxious Thoughts   55
7. Joy   65
8. Waiting   71
9. Obedience   79
10. Relationships   89
11. Healing   101
12. Righteousness Of Christ   107
13. Biblical Femininity   113
14. Daily Declarations: 119

Dedicated to my dear husband, Ricky

Foreword

This is more than a collection of thoughts and writings—it is an invitation to every woman of faith to embark on a journey of discovery, wisdom, freedom, wonder, and hope. In these pages, Stacey shares powerful and uplifting truths that speak with both timeless relevance and timely clarity. Her words call women to stand firmly in faith and to be grounded in the purity, sanctity, stability, and truth that can only be found in Jesus Christ.

Faith is powerful, and those who possess it become powerful people. As you read, you'll quickly sense Stacey's intention: to turn your gaze toward God, to lift your head, to help live as an overcomer, and to call forth everything on God's heart for you. In a world where the secular and biblical worldviews have never been more at odds, this book is profoundly needed. We are living in a critical moment in history—a time when identity, purpose, and faith are being challenged, dismantled, and dismissed. Such shaking disrupts our foundations and can cause deep emotional and psychological distress, undermining our sense of safety, significance, and belonging. Many wander through life searching for something—or someone—to give meaning and direction. Unless we are willing to courageously address these issues, they will erode the very life God intends us to live.

This book invites us to wrestle with the real questions:

What lies are destroying us? Where do we turn when we feel lost? Is there a path to a better life, wiser decisions, and true contentment? Who has the authority to define our future? Where can we find healing and restoring grace? How can my faith grow larger and larger until no more lies or deceptions are able to overtake me?

One line from this book struck me deeply and, I believe, captures why these pages matter so much... Stacey said: "I certainly wish someone had taught me this when I was eighteen years old. I would have been a lot wiser much sooner in life."

In this honest, transparent, and vulnerable work, Stacey offers much-needed encouragement and affirmation—words that will strengthen your faith and fuel your Christian walk. She writes with compassion but does not shy away from speaking firm, uncompromised truth when it is needed. She addresses God's design, identity, and purpose for every woman, drawing courageously from her own life, struggles, and testimonies to help readers see how wonderful God's thoughts toward them truly are. She refuses to leave harmful or unbiblical thinking unchallenged, reminding us that every thought shapes our faith and influences what we believe about ourselves, others, and God. The fear of the Lord, she shows us, is the true test of character.

Throughout the book, you will notice that Stacey never shifts her focus away from Jesus. Her aim is fixed on the Father—the One who forms the life she calls women to embrace. Rich with Scripture, the book is pastorally caring, theologically grounded, and deeply relational. It reads like a mentor raising up daughters, a mother calling forth the best in her children, and a prophetic voice summoning women everywhere to rise in faith.

I wholeheartedly applaud Stacey for this new book. Writing it is a brave act, and it reflects the depth of its message. As her pastor for several years, I can testify to the sincerity of her faith, the integrity of her ministry, and the passion with which she lives for God. She is a devoted wife, a gracious mother, a faithful Christian, and a valued leader in our church community. She loves God deeply, believes Him wholeheartedly, and stands unwaveringly on His Word. She has witnessed His miracles in her own life and now shares her experiences, breakthroughs, and revelations with all who will listen.

I believe God will use Stacey and her ministry mightily in this generation and the next.

The principles in this book are life-giving and true. I encourage you to read it—and to return to it often. Keep it by your bedside, and let God speak to you through the wisdom He has entrusted to Stacey.

Nico Smit, Hobart, Tasmania, Australia
Pastor, Revivalist, Prophet, Apostle, Speaker and Author
Lead Pastor of RiverCity Church, Hobart
Council member or the Australian Prophetic Council

Introduction

For God so loved the world that he gave his one and only Son, that whoever believes in him shall not perish but have eternal life. (John 3:16)

God is love. His love for us made Him send His one and only Son so that He could pay the ultimate price for sin - our sin. Jesus defeated death so that in Him we are resurrected. He sent His Holy Spirit to lead us into the eternal things of God rather than worldly distractions. The good news of Jesus gives life to our bones. God's love and His word are life-giving and an encouragement for everyone who will believe.

The serpent still whispers lies in the ears of young women, just like he did in the Garden of Eden. "Did God really say that?" Many women fall into this trap of questioning the voice of God. When we don't stand strong in our identity as God's beloved daughters, we are easily tempted by evil. We begin questioning God's promises for our lives. Over time we begin doubting God. Rather than holding His truths as wisdom, we let our hearts be hardened. The truth of the matter is that we live in a fallen world, and a war is raging around us, whether we like it or not. It is a war for our souls. The sooner we realize this, the better.

The Bible is clear about our identities. Years ago, I was searching the world to find happiness, life and even purpose. I wish someone had told me that I could find purpose, identity and everything else when I seek His kingdom. Gaining understanding of God's heart for us helps navigate the rough paths of our lives. I have attempted to just scratch the surface of the depths of what He wants for us as women with this book. The scripture states that His thoughts for us are as many as the grains of sand on this earth. In this world of noise and distraction, let this book be your noise canceling headphones. Let it bring you closer to God, one page at a time.

It could have saved me many years of wandering, lost, confused and angry if someone had told me biblical truths boldly and bluntly. My heart for you is that you would believe in the finished work of Christ and understand that your life is hidden in Christ. My heart is for you to come closer to God in every possible aspect. Let this book draw you one step closer to the living word of God.

1

Fearfully And Wonderfully Made

I grew up in a Christian home. I learned about God and His Word early on in my life. But what I didn't know was that the Word was true for me too. I was always taught that verses like Jeremiah 29:11, were only for the Israelites.

"For I know the thoughts that I think toward you, says the Lord, thoughts of peace and not of evil, to give you a future and a hope." (NKJV)

God said this thousands of years ago to the people of Israel through Jeremiah. This Scripture was a piece of history. I had no clue that the same verse is true for me too. God thought about me. He had a purpose for me and a plan for me. He wanted to give me a future. You see, I was taught that the Bible was a history book, and it didn't have anything to say about the life that I live now.

The scripture states that God never changes (Hebrews 13:8). It says that His Word is alive and active. God is not bound by time, and therefore His Word and His promises are not bound by time. It applied to the Israelites yesterday and it applies to you today.

"Fear not I have redeemed you, I have called you by your name. You are mine." (Isaiah 43:1, NKJV)

A powerful and intimate statement: "You are mine." The price has been paid. You have been redeemed and you are His. What a privilege to be known as God's. I have seen Christians go through life not grasping this powerful truth. The result? They live and die in bondage. And they pass on their bondage to the next generations. I have meditated on this verse for so long and I still do. This is the truth, and truth is what sets us free from any kind of bondage.

"I praise You, because I am fearfully and wonderfully made." (Psalm 139:14)

This verse speaks volumes about how intricately God has woven us. His thoughts toward us are precious, and they outnumber the grains of sand on the earth.

Do you know who knows how many grains of sand there are on the earth? God does – He knows the exact number of grains of sand on Earth and His thoughts for you are more than that. How amazing! The idea that the Creator of this world and this universe, the one who has made the things that are seen and unseen, the author of what we know and what we don't, thinks about you. He considers you valuable.

When I meditate on this, I cannot fathom the love that He has for me. It is safe to say, this lifetime is not enough to know God's love intimately. But we can understand His grace and love through His Word.

The Bible makes it clear what God thinks about us and how often we are in His thoughts. He calls us His bride, His royal people, co-heirs with Christ. We are His beloved, His sons and daughters, we are His, His chosen people. He speaks to our identity through the Scriptures so that we can understand our authority. When we are secure in our identity, no enemy can plant a negative seed in our hearts.

The enemy always comes against our identity. When we don't know who we are or who we are called to be, we are in a vulnerable place. The world constantly tells us who we should be. Society constantly tries to shift our focus from who we truly are to questioning our true identity.

Whatever place you are in, whether you have been bullied and wounded, whether you have sinned and are ashamed, whether you have been disobedient, lack self-esteem, or whether you despise yourself because of something that makes you believe you are unlovable, I want to affirm this to you: God loves you no matter what. He sent His only Son to die for you so that you can live eternally. What amazing love!

Young women struggle with the idea of being likable. I have been in a place where I would do anything to please people. I became what I thought people would like and appreciate. And when people rejected me, I felt like I wasn't good enough. I spent many years thinking that the reason people didn't accept me was because there must be something wrong with me. As a result, I strayed away from what God wanted me to be. This is an extremely slick attack of the enemy especially against young women. It benefits the enemy when we never recognize who we are. If we never know our true identity, we will never know our true purpose. And if we never seek our purpose, we will never be a threat to the enemy.

As a Man Thinketh in His Heart

Our thoughts play a powerful role in our mindsets. The Scripture says in Proverbs 23:7, *"For as a man thinks in his heart, so is he."* One thing that we have to realize is that the enemy knows the Scriptures. He has thousands of years of experience forming strategic arrows against us. He has an age advantage over us, and he has studied us and forged weapons that will work against us if we are not careful.

Thoughts are one of those weapons.

Think about the enemy as an archer constantly firing flaming arrows at us. One of those arrows is enough to take us out. The arrows are thoughts. If we accept just one of those thoughts and meditate on it, it has the power to change our mindset and therefore change our perspective on both people and life.

It took me an awfully long time to break out of my patterns of thinking. I had to read a lot of books and meditate on the Word of God every morning and night in order to change the way my mind was set to think. If someone had given me this wisdom from the Scriptures sooner in life, I would have been able to shift my mindset much earlier on. Just like Romans 12:1 says, I would have been completely transformed to the point of being unrecognizable much earlier in life.

Made in the Image of God.

While growing up, many of my friends were conventionally pretty. Unbeknownst to them, I developed a quiet contempt for myself. I despised my appearance - my skin, my height, even my hair - none of it measured up to what I considered to be pretty. I did not like myself at all. And because of this, I had low confidence and self-esteem issues. I could not speak up. I was shy. I always thought I was not enough and no matter what I did, I would never measure up.

Many young women live under this oppression. They believe that they aren't enough. And whatever they do, they cannot measure up. All because they believe the lies of comparison just like I did.

There are no two fingerprints in this entire world of almost eight billion people that are alike. Not even that of twins. Every person is uniquely made. There is deep thought and purpose behind the existence of every human being that has ever lived. And God knows each one of us deeply and intimately. He knows that we are unique, and He understands our deep need to be loved uniquely. But first we need to recognize our uniqueness in God to understand how God has a unique purpose grafted into us, just like our fingerprints. The Bible states that we are made in His image. (Genesis 1:26-27).

When God calls us, He first restores us completely. He restores our identity and however minuscule our hatred of ourselves may seem in the grand scheme of things, God cares about our view of ourselves.

"And have put on the new self, which is being renewed in knowledge in the image of its Creator." (Colossians 3:10)

If our faith and belief is in Christ. Then we have put on Christ. When God began to talk to me about my identity, He made sure to restore my view of myself. And He used prophetic words and dreams from other people to speak to me. People I did not know would come to me and tell me how they thought I was beautiful.

I knew it was God. I knew He needed me to be whole in every area of my life. He knew that the enemy could use this weapon against me if I was not fully restored. If you are suffering under this same mindset, be encouraged - God cares about your view of yourself. He wants to build you up. And because you have Christ in you, the hope of Glory, you will always be one step ahead of the enemy. The Holy Spirit will guide you and make sure of this.

Being made in the image of God is about your character, righteousness, behavior, relationships and everything that makes you who you are. God refines each and every aspect of your heart and mind while He is making you into who He created you to be. And in the process, you become a useful vessel for Himself and others.

In other words, every aspect of you, including how you relate to the world and those around you is God's business. He is a personal God.

As you get to know Him and draw near to Him, He refines and restores every corner of you. As He peels different layers off you, He reveals your true identity. Fully knowing your identity is what makes you confident in your authority as a believer, and as a young woman. It is then impossible for the world to redefine what God has already defined for you.

God has already provided us assurance and safety in His Word. As we understand our own identity and authority, we can rest in Him and His Word. Psalm 23:1 says, *"The Lord is my shepherd."* When I read this verse, I imagine myself following God around as He leads the way. I imagine that as I am His, He is my shepherd. He sometimes carries me and sometimes has to come looking for me when I get myself into trouble as I stray away from Him. But as His Word clearly states, *"The Lord is my shepherd."*

I can always rely on my Shepherd to give me an identity, to provide for me, to give me shelter and refuge in my time of need, and therefore I shall not want. I shall not want anything else.

I am His and when I obey Him and follow Him, I fulfill every purpose that He has for me. I know I was designed for something and as I walk with God, I can rest assured that I am walking in my identity and purpose. As I walk with Him, I know that even if I walk through the valley of the shadow of death, I am safe and secure with God.

Knowing your identity does not mean that the enemy will never come near you or attack you. He will keep shooting His fiery arrows to take you down. He will use every weapon in his arsenal to make sure that you forget who you are and become insecure so that you can never function fully in your purpose, and your destiny is derailed. But knowing that we have the great and mighty God on our side, Who not only loves us, but cares about us and calls us His own, makes us immune to the enemy's weapons. His word, as we read, understand and stand on it, becomes the shield against his fiery arrows.

I love the movie, "The Lion King." At first glance, it looks like a simple animated movie. But it has so many moments we can all relate to. Especially pertaining to our Kingdom identity and walking in purpose. Simba runs away and is living in the wilderness, surviving on worms. Despite having friends and food, he starts questioning whether that was the place he was supposed to be. Was that the food he was supposed to eat? He was an only heir to His father's kingdom. It was only when he stepped into his true identity as the king's son that he was able to conquer Scar's plan and take back the kingdom that was rightfully his. We can enter into our promise only when we understand our identity in Christ. Our identity is hidden in Christ as we are saved through grace by faith.

The Word says that without knowledge, people perish. We are not meant to go on in this life living like most everyone else. We are not just meant for a job or whatever the world considers important. We are meant for a purpose which God has planned for us and given us our identity for. Without coming into the knowledge of our true identity, we perish. In other words, God considers it a serious matter that we know who we are in Him. Just like a soul perishes eternally without salvation, we live unfulfilled and frustrated lives when we don't understand who we truly are.

PRACTICAL STEPS

I want to encourage you to ask God what He says about you. Have a conversation with Him about your identity. It may not unfold immediately, but it will as you surrender your will and your heart to Him. As He shows you, write it down on a piece of paper or a sticky note or a journal. Make it your lighthouse or a guiding light to where God wants you to go. When you let God make a plan for you, He directs your steps.

Find out what Bible verses fit your identity the best. Write them down on a sticky note and stick it somewhere visible and declare them every day to rewire your brain to come into alignment with your identity according to what God says about you.

REFLECTIONS

1. Are there any insecurities that hold you back? What are they? What does God say about your insecurities?

2. Have you asked God what He thinks of you?
   If not, ask Him and journal it.

2

Promises

"God is not human, that he should lie, not a human being, that he should change his mind. Does he speak and then not act? Does he promise and not fulfill?" (Numbers 23:19)

The Bible is full of God's promises and His heart for us. He promised the Israelites He would take them to the land of milk and honey. He promised Abraham he would be given a son. He promised His disciples He would rise to life on the third day. He has promised us that He has come to give us life and life abundantly. He has said that He can do exceedingly and abundantly more than we could ever ask or imagine.

Whatever is the wildest and greatest thing you can imagine for yourself, God can top it. He can one-up it. I find comfort in knowing that the God of this entire universe would personally do something that is not even in my wildest imagination.

God is a God of promises. He is faithful. He never fails. He fulfills everything He promises. He is not a man that He shall lie. In fact, it is written, no word that comes out of God's mouth returns to Him until it does what He sends it to do. We can trust His Word, which says God fulfills all His promises. He is faithful and true.

He fulfills His promises in ways that are far outside the box. When the Jews were waiting for a King to deliver them, He came as a carpenter and delivered them, paving the way to eternal life. Isn't that something?! His ways are truly higher than our ways. With the birth and death of Jesus, God fulfilled more than three hundred prophecies from the old testament. Jesus is the ultimate example of God fulfilling His promise to mankind.

These same promises are available to us. They can come as a word someone gives to us (which aligns with the Scriptures), or He can speak to us Himself through the Scriptures. When God gives a promise, just know that not a single word from the mouth of God returns void. It always does what it's sent out to do. If He promises you something, He is more than able to fulfill it for you. It may not come immediately. It may tarry and take time. But every word is fulfilled.

Dreams

As a young woman, I had many dreams. In fact, I had many plans. I had a plan for my career, my marriage and everything in between. But our plans are never God's plans. In my dreaming, one main ingredient was missing - God. I wasn't dreaming with God. I wasn't planning with Him. I wasn't submitting my plans to God. The truth is, I wasn't even considering Him and His plans for me. I was placing my bets on my future capacity to provide for myself and fulfill my own dreams. I was naive. But I was never taught how to do these things with God. I just thought that we plan and then when things don't work out, we pray. If only someone had stopped me in my tracks, I would have learned early on that only God is the orchestrator and fulfiller of our dreams.

Make no mistake, God does fulfill the desires of our hearts. But sometimes, our desires may lack the right motivation which may cause many delays and detours. His Word states that when we delight in the Lord and follow His commands, He is more than faithful to fulfill the desires of our heart. The thing is, when we are consumed by following what God has commanded, our dreams automatically align with His will. When we walk in the Spirit, our desires come into synchronicity with His. As an old hymn puts it, "And the things of this world grow strangely dim, in the light of this Glory and grace."

When we walk in our purpose and align our desires with His, Holy Spirit testifies His promises to us - sometimes through His word as we read it or through others who faithfully share with us when they hear from God for us.

A simple yet powerful scripture like Jeremiah 29:11 helps us to see ourselves from God's perspective – how He thinks about us. Romans 8:28 also shows us that He has a plan for us and that He works out everything for our good. God's Word speaks to us in any situation we may find ourselves, and He makes sure to meet us there and comfort us through Scripture, prophetic dreams and words, and sometimes through the goodness of God's people.

When we lose strength, He promises us strength. (Philippians 4:13)

He promises to fight our battles and go before us to win the battle for us.

He promises to be strong in us when we are weak.

He promises us salvation and eternal life.

He promises us that He will come back for us riding on the clouds.

He promises us love, compassion, grace, mercy, righteousness, and above all He promises us reconciliation with God.

He says He understands that we are made from dust. And He remembers it.

I want to encourage every reader to find a promise in the Scripture that pertains to your situation. For example, if you are going through heartbreak, you can rest assured that the Lord is close to the brokenhearted and to those with a contrite heart. (Psalms 34:18). Believe that God heals all our wounds, as the Scripture says, 'by His stripes we are healed' (Isaiah 53:5). Even when the wounds are invisible to others, God sees every part of us, and He lovingly heals and restore us.

When I felt like everything in my life was falling apart and nothing would ever be the same, God very clearly gave me a scripture.

".. to bestow on them the crown of beauty instead of ashes, the oil of joy instead of mourning, and a garment of praise instead of a spirit of despair. They will be called the oaks of righteousness, a planting of the Lord for the display of his splendour." (Isaiah 61:3)

What a verse to proclaim! It is like God is in the business of making beauty from ashes. I claimed this verse every day until I felt God guiding me to a different season in my life. I speak Psalm 91 daily over my children, as a prayer of protection. By doing this, we speak the reality before it manifests. That is what every promise of the Lord is for us - yes and amen!

Renewal of Our Mind

Do not conform to the pattern of this world but be transformed by the renewing of your mind. (Romans 12:2)

This world has a pattern. The pattern of this world is to elevate everything that is unholy as holy, and to despise everything that is holy as rigid and unnecessary. We can all fall into the trap of conforming to the world in one way or another. The trap doesn't look like a trap. For example, having friends that constantly gossip and putting others down. You may have always had those friends around, but the Scripture suggests that *"Blessed are those who do not sit in the company of mockers."* (Psalm 1:1).

There are real blessings attached to that verse, which are often diminished and lost because of the lack of knowledge. Again, as the Scripture says, because of lack of knowledge, people perish. It's not just about blessings, but about but by confirming to the unbiblical standards, we are slowly but surely compromising on the Biblical standards which ought to be above everything else.

The enemy even uses culture to induce anxiety, worries and other issues in us in order to diminish our identity. God asks us to cast our cares upon Him. But we so often forget that God is interested in our healthy hearts and minds. He is interested in every detail of our lives.

I realized early on in my life that we are in a battle. Whether we want to or not. Whether we stay still and do nothing or do something. Whether we like it or not, we are in a spiritual battle, and it rages around us 24/7. I decided to fight my battle, not just with fervent prayers but also Scriptures. I used the Word of God to fight the thoughts that came as arrows against me. I used to think that beauty was everything, and I did not have it. But the Scriptures say that I am fearfully and wonderfully made. If I am made wonderfully and in the image of God, how could the way I look be any less than any other person! God didn't make a mistake when He made me.

I had a very real conversation with God in which He clearly said, *"Beauty is fleeting but the woman who worships the Lord is to be praised." (Proverbs 31:30, ESV)*

Stand on the Word and fight the good fight because the enemy is fighting to keep you blind to the promises of God. Something as simple as just standing by while others are mocking someone can cost you a blessing in your life. Which is why it is in our favor to know what God has promised us. He has promised salvation and so much more that needs to be dug out like a treasure so we can make it a weapon in the spiritual fight going on around us. And when you find a promise or a word, make it your own. Stand on it, claim it for yourself daily. Live like the Word says. Become what the promise wants you to become. Speak it every day. Act like everything is already in your favor because the word that God gave you says so. Let your desires be aligned with God's desires so that you can see every promise fulfilled in your life.

Faith

Hebrews 11:1 states that faith is the substance of things unseen. A substance is real, physical matter which is tangible (Google). What this verse implies is that faith is tangible. It is not just felt but acted upon like a physical thing. Faith is the reality of that which is not yet seen. By faith, what is unseen can become seen. Faith doesn't say that God will do it. Rather it says that God has already done it. God has already fulfilled all the promises that He gave me.

Sometimes holding on to faith may seem like a season of waiting. But God utilizes every season of waiting to either draw us closer to him or draw us closer to His plans for us. Understand God is always on time. He is never late or early. Everything happens according to God's timetable. There is time for everything under the sun.

My daughter is three, and whenever she is hungry, she wants to eat her food piping hot. Her focus is only on the food that has been prepared for her and not on how it may burn her mouth. She has had a couple of incidents where she has burned her mouth because she was too eager to eat. She has now learnt to wait before eating her food if it's too hot. Waiting is just God protecting us, just like I protect my daughter from burning her mouth by asking her to wait.

He fulfills His promises to us, not in our time but in His time, which is perfect. It may seem frustrating when you're a new Christian or a young Christian. When we have a history with God, it makes it easier to trust Him and His timing. But understand that all the waiting becomes a testimony sooner than we realize.

When I meditate on the promises of God, I always think about the woman with the issue of blood. An outcast woman, someone who wasn't allowed to mix with people, heard about Jesus. She had exhausted all her money in order to find a cure. Even that didn't take her faith away. After twelve years of affliction, she hears about a man who performs healings and miracles. Without a shadow of doubt in her mind, she picks herself up, hiding her face from others, pushing through the crowds and touching others even when she is untouchable, she finally manages to touch the hem of his garment.

According to the law, if she wasn't successful and was caught before being able to touch the hem of Jesus' robe, she would have been stoned to death. She was not allowed in the city, let alone among a huge crowd of people where everyone was touching everyone else. She found something inside of her that was bigger than the fear of death. Perhaps, she was too tired of her affliction.

We know the reason why she took such a risk. Jesus revealed it. It was her faith that made her well. So, what did she put her faith in? A faith that allowed her to be so bold that she could risk death. She heard a man named Jesus who healed people. She aligned her promise with her faith. She put her faith in the One who promised healing. Not in the promise itself, but in the Giver of the promise. "If only I could touch the hem of HIS garment."

As the Scripture states, we only need faith the size of a mustard seed. But just holding a mustard seed in our hands wouldn't do anything. A seed is useful only when it is planted. You can keep it safely in a cabinet or even a treasure chest somewhere, but it won't do anything. Plant that mustard seed size faith in the person of Jesus. The one who gives the promise. The one who fulfills His promise A firm and planted faith not only takes risks like the woman with the issue of blood but is also obedient in the face of fears and trials, just like the faith of the disciples.

When Jesus called Simon and Andrew, His very first disciples, He promised to make them "fishers of men." I am quite sure neither of them understood what Jesus meant. Will they fish men from the ocean? Will they be trainers of fishermen? Will they catch more fishes then men? Even though we now know what Jesus meant by it, there was a lot of uncertainty about the invitation. But both Simon and Andrew followed Jesus anyway.

Jesus paired their callings, their identities to a promise. Therefore, even when they didn't understand what Jesus meant at the time, they followed Him without looking back. In that moment, they understood that the 'deep' of Jesus was calling the 'deep' within them and they decided to put their faith in the person of Jesus just like the woman who touched the hem of His garment.

Whatever the season might be, faith when combined with promise, becomes a substance of strength inside of us.

Speaking Truth Over Us

I have often heard adults say many negative things to their kids or the kids around them. There are certain bosses and mangers at work that speak negatively over us. There are situations when our parents, peers and friends speak certain negative words over us. They might not blatantly curse you. Although they may be well meaning, the words may attack our sense of self-worth. Words like, "but what if you fail?" "you're not smart enough to pull that off," "you don't believe that thing can actually happen to you, right?" etc. etc.

When I learned this truth, I realized how much weight I was carrying. Words carry the power to wear us down. These seemingly insignificant things can throw us off course in our destiny for an exceptionally long time. It can bring unnecessary delays and detours. It can deter us from walking into our purpose.

The challenge is to identify such words that have become a part of our identities. Bring everything to the feet of Jesus. Let him plant a seed of love inside of you so that you can see yourself as He sees you. Slowly, but surely, it becomes easier to believe in the promises that God gives us as we let Him purge us of the negative words we carry inside ourselves.

One practical key that I have used over the years is whenever a thought arises in my mind that does not align with God's plan for me, I reject the thought in Jesus' name. I find what God has promised me in the Scriptures instead and speak it over myself again and again until the thought completely vanishes. It takes time, but we eventually fall into the pattern of meditating on the promises, rather than the word-curses spoken over us by others or ourselves.

I have learnt that in order to believe in our promises, we must renew our mind and think about what is good and lovely and God honoring.

Prayer is another weapon in our arsenal. It brings heaven to Earth and changes our circumstances. Intentional prayers are not just a list of requests but are intimate conversations that bring us closer to Him. Leave room for the Holy Spirit to speak into your heart as you sit in the presence of the Lord. Let communication be a two-way street. Pray each and every promise with faith.

REFLECTIONS

1. What is the toughest season of life you've been through that felt like a wilderness season or a waiting season? How did you manage to cope in this season? What was the lesson you ultimately learned when you got out of that season?

2. What did the season of waiting teach you about God?

3. What promises has God given you pertaining to your future or current situation?
   If you are not sure about His promise to you, sit with Him and ask Him to reveal His promise to you.

3

Tethered Heart

"......so that Christ may dwell in your hearts through faith." (Ephesians 3:17)

The writer of Proverbs states that out of our hearts flow all the issues of life. A heart that has turned away from the Lord and is not anchored in the love of Christ, becomes callous. A callous heart is insensitive and even cruel towards others. Which is the complete opposite to the heart that Christ gives us - a compassionate and soft heart. A servant heart. A heart which is inclined towards the worship of our Creator.

A heart that is anchored in Christ is anchored in Truth. The only truth that satisfies our soul to the point that no lies can penetrate. But a heart that isn't tethered to Christ, sways with every lie. It takes on all the burdens of trauma, lies, betrayal and everything in-between, and is exhausted. We may then become easily manipulated by the lies of the culture around us.

An untethered heart makes you more like the man who builds his house on the sand, thinking it will survive the storms of life. A wise man knows the value and necessity of a strong and firm foundation on which to build a house.

My kids have blocks that they can stack on each other. They cannot build a proper house, but they love to stack the blocks on top of each other. A three-year-old doesn't understand that the foundation needs to be strong in order for it to bear the load of the world's tallest block building. And we all know what happens eventually. Building our house on the love of Christ and His sacrifice for our salvation is when we can truly start building our lives on a firm foundation.

Abide in Him

He who abides in me and I in him, bears much fruit. For without me you can do nothing. (John 15:5, NKJV)

Abide is an old English word which means, await, remain, dwell, continue, endure. To abide in Jesus means to dwell in Him, Without abiding in Jesus, we can do nothing. Ephesians 3:17 states that we can dwell in Christ through faith. Faith will keep us in Him. I have discovered that our secret place is the best place to learn to dwell in Jesus. When we communicate with Him, we begin to rely on Him. Though it has been a gradual process for me, I am now in a place where my heart is completely tethered in Christ. I know I can rely on Him for everything. In chaos or calm, I have faith that nothing is too difficult for Him to handle.

The secret place is our shelter where we can abide in Him and just remain with Him. Getting in the Word is the best way to know Him. Ignoring the Word keeps us away from the truth. Holy spirit communicates through the Word even in unlikely situations. He uses the Word to comfort us and refresh us.

I love to read the Psalms and dwell on those chapters for a long time. King David bares his soul and his emotions to the Lord. He is so emotionally intelligent and aware that he tells the Lord exactly what he is going through. It is like he is talking to a friend. It is so easy for him to tell the Lord everything. He never blames God for his circumstances. But at the end of almost every Psalm he's written, he is found praising God. His relationship with God is so profound that even when his own son dies, he chooses to praise the Lord. Even when his other son chases him to take his life, he chooses to praise God.

I believe this is what abiding looks like. Baring our soul to God without blaming our situation on Him and then praising Him because God is almighty and He can use anything for our good. This is what our secret place must look like.

No matter what our situation looks like. There may be sin in our lives. Maybe no one wants to be around us because of our circumstances. There might be unusual warfare which has increased in your life at this moment. Maybe it's just a war of thoughts - something that you're battling with in your head. Whatever it may be, lay it all down at the feet of Jesus. Like the woman pouring out the alabaster jar at the feet of Jesus, let your worship become an alabaster jar even when you don't feel like doing it.

Just going into the secret place and abiding in His presence, relieves us of all the muck and mire that we may have carried for a long time. Anchor yourself to His presence and His Word.

Rooted in Christ

Whenever a seed is planted, it germinates and grows its roots first. Whether it is a cumin seed or a mustard seed or an apricot or peach seed, the first thing to happen during the process of germination is the seed breaks, and then the roots grow. After this process, it takes some time before we see a little green shoot sprouting from the ground. Then, as it continues to grow on the outside, it spreads its root even deeper. I have roses in my back yard, and they bloom every year without fail. I have never once had to water them or do anything for them apart from some occasional pruning. The secret is in their roots. Their roots are so deep that they get all their nutrition from the ground itself, and the flowers are proof of it.

Our relationship with our Lord Jesus Christ should look the same. Being in the Word and understanding the unwavering love of Christ towards us is when we find ourselves building on the foundation of Christ. It is the place true worship stems from.

"Therefore, as you received Christ Jesus the Lord, so walk in him, rooted and built up in Him and established in faith, just as you were taught, abounding in thanksgiving." (Colossians 2:6-7, ESV)

The apostle Paul shows the steps in order. First, you receive Christ, then you get rooted and walk with Him, and after that comes the rest of the growth. Then comes being established in faith. He also states these things were taught - the people were discipled in their walk with Christ. I want to encourage you to find a connect group or a youth group or simply a woman who is older than you (spiritually mature and not just older in age) to help you walk out your faith in Christ. It helps you to not only get rooted in Christ but also helps you to be accountable. Accountability like this can help you build a stronger root system on which your whole life can be established. Discipleship is like a water system for the roots.

When our hearts are centered in Christ, we aren't moved by anything else. When I was little, my father used to teach us the truth of God's Word every day. And it happened for a long time, from when I was a little girl until I became a teenager. The foundation of truth was laid. And I will always be thankful to him that no storm can shake away my love for God. Nothing can take away my faith in Christ because of the root system that was watered so early on in my life. That doesn't mean that I have not strayed along the way. Even though I am not proud to confess it, I have given in to many temptations in life. And sometimes I still do. They aren't that big but are sneaky. Like talking behind someone's back. It seems harmless in the moment but afterwards the Holy Spirit always brings conviction. Because it is not what my mouth was made for. It was made to worship God and to praise. I then always find myself alone and repenting before God so that I am in right standing with Him. The trick is to have a system to avoid situations like that - steering the conversation away from a person to God has always worked for me in these circumstances.

Being rooted in Christ doesn't mean that we will always make the right decisions. We may fail. But when our hearts are tethered in Christ, we become more and more inclined towards holiness rather than falling for worldly temptations.

"Trust in the Lord with all your heart and lean not on your own understanding." (Proverbs 3:5)

In comparison to God, our understanding is limited. And understandably so. God is an infinite God while we are finite human beings. It is by design; we have no understanding of certain mysteries that surround the universe. But we can always trust the one Who is the creator of this universe. The One who created time and decided to put us inside of time and space. In doing so, He has given us the greatest gift - Himself. We do not trust in our circumstances but in the goodness of Christ. Leaning on our own understanding is pride. But trusting in the Lord is humility. It shows our understanding that we cannot grow even an inch of our hair by worrying about it. Moreover, leaning on oneself creates anxiety and depression - extremely useful tools of the enemy in this day and age. We become anxious because we are aware of our shortcomings. We know that it is impossible to establish anything by ourselves, let alone the salvation of our souls. Consequently, more people in the world are on medications now than there have ever been. It is not the discovery of the medications that has led to this state of humanity, but the awareness of one's finite state.

God provides us with wisdom through His Word. How blessed are we to have a God who wants our anxiety! How blessed are we to have a God who asks us just to trust Him so that He can take care of everything for us! So, to me, it is wisdom to trust in the Lord and give everything to Him.

Guard your Heart

"Above all else, guard your heart for everything you do flows from it." (Proverbs 4:23, NIV)

Everything flows from the heart. All of our emotions, whether they are positive or negative, are felt in the heart. Whenever we feel heartbreak, or any other intense emotion, our chest becomes heavy. Any intense emotion that flows directly from our heart has the ability to permanently affect it. Our hearts can become dead, callous and cruel, and they can also become bitter. Therefore, we are clearly instructed to guard our hearts. Isn't it amazing that all we need to live a fruitful and purposeful life, is already given to us in the Word?

But how do we guard our hearts? We guard our hearts with the Word. We immerse our hearts in the Scriptures for it to become a wall of protection around our hearts. Every lie and every emotion can be tackled with the truth of His word. I am not suggesting you run away from your emotions. By all means we need to feel them, but at the same time we cannot choose to dwell on our emotions. We need to speak to our hearts to come into alignment with the word of God. The truth of Scripture helps us to deal with every emotion in such a way that it does not corrupt our heart. The Word becomes a cleaning agent, wiping away all the muck and mire from our hearts.

Bringing God into every trauma, every pain, every hurt, every betrayal and into every deep place that we have hidden from ourselves is what makes the heart clean. These are the things that not only corrupt the heart but prevent us from walking in our authority as a follower of Christ. I would rather bring all the filth of my heart to God than not be able to walk with the Lord in full authority. It might be a sin we are hiding from. By confessing it to the Lord and speaking His truth over us, we take the power out of that sin. However small it may be, bring it to the Lord and see how He changes our heart with His love and His truth.

"And the peace which surpasses all understanding, will guard your hearts and your minds through Christ Jesus." (Philippians 4:7, NKJV)

When we bring all our troubles to God, He gives us His peace, and this peace cannot be found in the natural realm. Rather, God gives us a peace which is supernatural. And this peace, which He offers, has the ability to be a guard for our hearts. Think about Jesus sleeping when there was a storm and the disciples were afraid for their lives. Jesus was fully man then, but He wasn't affected by the storm that was raging outside. He wasn't affected by the very thing that threatened His own disciples. That is what the "peace that surpasses all understanding" looks like. When we are in Christ, this supernatural peace is what becomes the guard around our hearts. Imagine not being moved by outer circumstances but being at total peace with Jesus and His love for us.

Jesus's sleep was disturbed by His disciples, and He calls out their lack of faith. That means that through our faith in God we receive peace. Now, being reprimanded by Jesus for my lack of faith is not what I would want. But we learn and we grow. How many times have we acted in total panic because we lost our faith? I have done it countless times. I have freaked out over situations that looked out of my control. And we all do. But the only thing we need to remind ourselves is that Jesus is in our boat. And when our heart is anchored in this truth, no storms can shake us or move us. Peace becomes our guard.

Peace is not just a feeling. Because feelings are fleeting. They change. But the peace offered to us is a Kingdom of peace that reigns over us. Jesus is the Prince of peace. We do not have Kings and Princes without a kingdom or a realm. Hence, peace is a kingdom that Jesus offers to us. When you are under the reign of peace, it guards your heart. It allows you to keep your heart tethered in the reality of Jesus Christ as the ruler.

Living in Christ

"I have been crucified with Christ and I no longer live but Christ lives in me." (Galatians 2:20)

If we have been crucified with Christ, then all the desires of the flesh should be crucified. Anything that is not Jesus or does not glorify God must be crucified. This is easier said than done. Does your insecurity about your grades glorify God? Does lying to your parents or friends or teachers glorify God? Does sneaking out at night glorify God? Does being a people-pleaser glorify God?

Jude 1:23 states, "Hate even a garment stained by flesh." A strong aversion to the things of this world comes only when the flesh has been crucified, just like Paul states. When Jesus lives inside of us, we do the things that glorify the Father because that is what Jesus modeled when He was on this Earth. He did the things that He saw His father do. Being Christlike is not just a statement but a greater call. A call to live against the tide. While your friends are partying, you are at home studying or spending time with your family. When your friends prioritize ungodly music, you set your heart on worshiping God. When your peers go out drinking after work, you choose to go to a Bible study or a small group. When others choose to sleep in on Sundays, you choose to be in the house of God. These simple things make us rebel against secular culture. You will hear things like you are still young or you only live once or live a little or get a life. People may call you a Jesus freak.

Going against the tide, especially when you are still forming your relationship with Jesus, is tough. If you are a people-pleaser, it is even tougher. But when Christ lives in you, it becomes easy to choose godly over ungodly. When you heart is tethered in Christ, you will choose to love these people and not conform to them.

As a grown woman and a mother of three, I realize now that the road to heaven is really narrow. It is only you and Jesus. I often imagine this road as a bridge over a valley. And this bridge does not have any railings. And the valley is filled with all kinds of distractions. Worldly pleasures like money, sex, alcohol, drugs and emotions like pride and ambition, and all the things that do not glorify the Lord even a bit. But you have the hand of Jesus to hold onto and walk the road. Like Paul says, keeping your eyes focused on what is important. It is no easy feat. But we have the comfort of knowing that the Christ inside of us, is what we are putting our faith in.

Walking with Jesus, is all about making history with God. In the beginning, it may not be easy to entrust any situation to him because you do not know how it will turn out. As humans we have an inherent need to control everything around us according to our will. Hence, it is hard to put everything at the feet of Jesus and completely rely on him. It takes time. The more you spend time in His Word and in the secret place, the more you familiarize yourself with His character. And the more familiar you become with His character, the greater the chances are that you will trust Him in any given situation.

The Scriptures teach us that God is good. But the experience of His goodness only comes when we are in a murky situation and God shows His goodness by standing with us, comforting us, teaching us through the hard days and then taking us out of it. That is when we taste His goodness. When we have an experience of it, we are more likely to put our faith in His goodness next time. And that is how we build a history with God. Slowly it becomes second nature to us, to trust in God and lean not in our own understanding. I have reached a point where I don't even consider my own understanding about any situation. I just trust and give it to Him. The One who is in me is greater than the one who is in the world.

New Creation

"Therefore, if anyone is in Christ, he is a new creation; Old things have passed away; behold, all things have become new." (2 Corinthians 5:17, NKJV)

For anything new to come, the old has to go. Unless the old completely goes away, the new cannot come. Hence, when we receive salvation, we, by faith, believe that everything inside of us is now new. We are a new creation, which means the way we were before, we aren't now. We start believing this and living our life out of this belief, working out our salvation every day.

The enemy will often tempt us with condemnation. We will hear this voice inside our heads reminding us of our sins that we have been forgiven of. It will make us question our salvation. Are our sins really washed away? Have you ever seen a newborn? Do you think they wonder if they are really born or are still inside the womb? Or a butterfly, do you think that it thinks of crawling on the leaves again when it can fly? Thinking about our old self and how we were is somewhat like this. You may have been a rebel or a liar or an outcast or a gang member, or you may have cheated on a test, gossiped about a friend, vandalized a property, but the moment you decided to follow Christ and repent and turn away, God erases all your sins. It says in the Scriptures that He remembers them no more. He separates our sins from us as far the east is from the west.

When we become a new creation in Jesus, our thoughts become new, our behavior changes and we change. Therefore, any condemnation that is brought against us is a lie. The thoughts sound like our own voice, but they are planted by the enemy to erase the work of Christ. To make us forget that we indeed are a new creation in Christ. They become a trap to keep our hearts anxious. Instead, we need to let our hearts rest in the reality of how we are new and nothing from our past can affect us because of the blood of Jesus, and all our sins are washed clean by His sacrifice.

"For by grace you have been saved through faith. And this is not your own doing; it is a gift of God, not a result of works so that no one may boast." (Ephesians 2:8-9, ESV)

It is imperative to remind ourselves that we are saved by the grace of God and not by anything that we have done or are capable of doing. Even though these thoughts look innocent, all they do is plant a seed of doubt against the full and finished work of Christ. These thoughts, if not taken captive on time, have the ability to make us strive in our own strength to fight with condemnation. But the reality is that we aren't meant to fight with it. Rather just take the thought captive and remind ourselves of the Scripture that it is His grace and not our works that separate us from our sins. The whole point of grace is that we are given something that we do not deserve. We become new creations by grace.

It is God who loved us so much that He gave his one and only son for us and nothing can separate us from that love. Paul says, *"For I am convinced, that neither life nor death, neither angels nor demons, neither the present nor the future, nor any powers, neither height nor depth, nor any-*

thing else in all creation will be able to separate us from the love of God that is in Christ Jesus our Lord." (Romans 8:38–39, NIV)

How reassuring it is to know that there is nothing that has the ability to keep God's love away from us. No condemnation brought against us can take God's love from us. Resting our hearts in this reality is what keeps it anchored. Anchored in the grace and love of Christ.

Initially, I struggled with this tactic of the enemy too. I've come to understand that when I allow thoughts of my past to diminish the finished work of Christ, I'm giving undue power and importance to the sin that once held me captive. Even though it is not the reality of the new me, the enemy tries his best to keep me trapped in the cycle of condemnation. Which is why taking every such thought captive before it takes us captive is of utmost importance.

REFLECTIONS

1. What makes you anxious the most? Journal it and give it to the Lord. Journal what God says about it.

2. Journal the last time your heart felt untethered from the Lord. Journal how you felt about the situation.
   Does this chapter make any difference to how you view your relationship with God?

3. How have you guarded your heart in the past?
   How will you guard your heart now?

4

Wisdom

Say to wisdom, "You are my sister," and call insight your intimate friend. (Proverbs 7:4, ESV)

I give each new year a name after asking the Holy Spirit what He wants me to spend my time learning about in that particular year. The year 2019 was my year of wisdom. I spent the entire year studying Proverbs and asking for wisdom. It is wise to keep wisdom as close as your sister. I am remarkably close to my sister, and I share every little detail of my life with her and vice versa. I am older than her, so she often comes to me for advice and more often than not, she trusts me and does what I advise her. Our relationship with wisdom should be like that. All the decisions we take need to first pass through the gateway of wisdom. The question is, what is wisdom? Proverbs 1:7 states, *"The fear of the Lord is the beginning of wisdom."*

It is the fear of the Lord where wisdom begins. It is wise to have reverential fear of Lord in every situation. King Solomon asked the Lord for wisdom and the Lord granted it to him. And it is said that there never was or has ever been a man as wise as King Solomon. We have social media now, so we know about all the intelligent people in the world.

We tend to notice all the knowledge and wisdom of the world and hear all about it because of the technological advances we have made. But King Solomon was known for his wisdom far and wide without any such technological advances.

It is said people used to visit him, especially to hear his wisdom and see it in action. An Egyptian queen, Queen Sheba, visited King Solomon and brought him gifts. His wisdom encompassed heavenly and earthly wisdom. It was reflected in his judgements and even the economic state of his Kingdom. Gold was extremely common in his era.

I do not think Solomon himself would have thought that wisdom would bring him fame and honor, not only among his people but among other nations as well.

So, how do we attain wisdom? Proverbs 4:7 states, *"The beginning of wisdom is this: Get wisdom."* And that is what King Solomon did. He got wisdom when he could. He asked for wisdom above all things.

"If any of you lacks wisdom, you should ask God, who gives generously to all without finding fault, and it will be given to you." (James 1:5)

Our God is a generous God. His generosity is reflected in every aspect of creation. He has already provided generously, by providing us with salvation through His son and moreover by sending His Holy Spirit to live within us. He shows His love generously every day - in every chirp of a bird, the first rays of the sun, in every colorful sunset and in every breath we take. Therefore, when we ask Him, He gives. When we ask for wisdom, He gives generously.

Getting good grades isn't wisdom. Choosing to spend time studying even when we don't feel like it, that's wisdom. The outcome of choosing wisdom is always good. This may be quite a simple example, but it can be applied to our day-to-day lives. Choosing to speak with kindness, thinking about others, putting others above ourselves, are some of the many ways we can exercise wisdom. Regret always follows when we fail to exercise wisdom.

God does not hold wisdom from us because of our faults or wrongdoings. He doesn't consider our failures at all. He knows we require wisdom, and it is His joy to give it to us when we ask. If more people asked for wisdom, there would be many more people like King Solomon.

"Judah and Israel lived in safety, from Dan to Beersheba, every man under his vine and his fig tree, all the days of Solomon." (1 Kings 4:25, ESV)

There were peace and safety during the reign of King Solomon. This speaks volumes about how he used his God-given gift in order to create a peaceful realm for every person who was in his kingdom. We can say that peace and safety are fruits of wisdom. James 3:17 states that the wisdom that comes from heaven is pure, peace loving, considerate, submissive, full of mercy, impartial and sincere.

Worldly wisdom creates division and wars, but heavenly wisdom creates peace and security. I have worked in a corporate environment where putting others down and being ruthless in competition is considered wisdom. How completely opposite to the teaching of God!

When you feel the urge to speak rashly, argue with someone who's hurt you, or humiliate them as they once did to you, you're not walking in Biblical wisdom. Biblical wisdom teaches us to show kindness and mercy to those who wrong us because it is like heaping burning coals on their heads. Humility is considered wisdom. Taming your tongue is wisdom. Showing accountability for your words as well as your actions is wisdom.

"The Spirit of the Lord will rest on him - the spirit of wisdom and understanding, the spirit of counsel and might, the spirit of the knowledge and fear of the Lord." (Isaiah 11:2)

Holy Spirit is the seven-fold spirit. We have the Holy Spirit inside of us which means that we have the Spirit of wisdom living inside of us. Jesus told His disciples in John 14 that Holy spirit will teach them everything. Hence Holy Spirit is not just a comforter and our helper but is also our teacher. He teaches us wisdom because He is made of wisdom. We can conclude that wisdom and understanding are a part of God. He sent it to us knowing fully well we will require it to live our lives on this earth.

Holy Spirit makes Jesus and the Word real to us. When we let Holy Spirit lead us, His wisdom guides us through sometimes treacherous and sometimes troublesome challenges. His wisdom is what helps us navigate through tough relationships and hard circumstances. When the Word becomes real in our life, we learn to live according to the wisdom of the Word with the help of Holy spirit.

Wisdom is essential for living a Christian life. Without it, we can so easily be led stray by the wisdom of this world. Rebelling against our parents or higher authority when we don't like what is being asked of us, is earthly wisdom. Honoring our parents and not despising their teaching and praying for those in authority is heavenly wisdom. Sometimes, respecting a curfew set by our parents may seem foolish to us and our peers, but obeying the boundaries set by them is wisdom.

I have been unwise and kept company with those who have altered my thoughts regarding the LGBTQAI community. I remember fighting with my father about how I couldn't believe God was good because how can He make a person a certain way and then ask them not to act on their desires. I literally had this exact argument with my father when I was eighteen years old. How foolish of me to think I can decide what God should do in order to be good! I was setting the standard of goodness for God because, according to me, His goodness wasn't good enough. I am glad that I am not that foolish anymore. I understand the innate desire in all of us to sin. It might be something different than indulging in homosexuality, but we are all born with an evil desire to sin. This is the reason we need to be born again.

God's goodness is not reflected in what He allows us to do. Yes, He has given us free will to make our own decisions, but what most of us forget is that every decision comes with its own consequences. Wisdom is in pursuing God to understand His will and His good purposes for us. God's goodness is reflected in what He saves us from doing and by His saving grace provides us with a way out of our sinful lives.

I certainly wish someone had taught me this when I was eighteen years old. I would have been a lot wiser much sooner in life. I was never encouraged to ask tough questions about life and about wisdom to live a Christian life well. Therefore, I always try my best to bring a Biblical perspective which can be helpful to someone who to be wise in their approach to life.

When I was studying Proverbs, I found wisdom for every aspect of life, be it spiritual, financial, natural or just wisdom for day-to-day life. It truly has everything we need to live a fruitful life.

"Wisdom is found in those who take advice." (Proverbs 13:10)

Taking advice is wisdom. If you think about it, it is counter cultural. "How dare you say anything to me!" is the normal response of most people when you try to give them advice. Even Socrates said, "I know that I know nothing." Now Socrates was a wise Greek philosopher in Plato's works, and this statement reflects his yearning to acquire knowledge. When someone thinks that they know everything, they don't desire to learn anymore. They never grow in wisdom because there is no desire for growth. There is no greater fool than the one who thinks he has acquired all knowledge.

Being teachable is wise. Wisdom is taking advice from those who have gone before you. Be aware, though, that bad advice is also a thing; some people may give you bad advice just to be on your good side, to stroke your ego or because they are envious of you. So, wisdom comes with discernment. It's wise to not ask just any random person for advice – we need to surround ourselves with people who can give us wise and Godly counsel.

When someone betrays us, or slanders our name for whatever reason, we may be tempted to retaliate in the same manner. Perhaps, you may plot to seek revenge, but God says, "Vengeance is mine." Letting God fight for us is the wisest decision in this situation.

Not all advice will bring about God's will for our lives - the discernment of the Holy spirit is necessary. Discernment helps you choose your advisers wisely.

"Walk with the wise and become wise for the companion of fools suffers harm." (Proverbs 13:20)

There is a saying in the secular world, "Show me the people you hang out with, and I will show you your future." If your friends are broke and living under a poverty mindset, the chances are that you will end up like them. If, however, the friends you hang out with believe in working hard you will be encouraged to do the same. Your future depends a lot on the people you choose to spend your time with. Godly friends will bring you closer to God, whereas worldly friends will draw you closer to all the pleasures of the world.

As you read this, you most likely know what types of people you surround yourself with. If your friends take you closer to your spiritual, financial and career goals, then you have surrounded yourself with the correct counsel. If not, then it is time to change who influences you.

"The statutes of the LORD are trustworthy making wise the simple." (Psalm 19:7)

The law of the Lord and all His commandments are what gives us wisdom. How can a simple man become wise? By following the written word of God. Proverbs 23:17 states that if there is wisdom in our hearts, God is glad. God has made it such that in order to live a fruitful life, a heart full of wisdom is necessary. And He is glad when we pursue wisdom with all our might because Godly wisdom is the peace that guards our hearts.

The Prodigal Son

The story of the prodigal son is a famous story used to illustrate salvation and God's unwavering love for us even after we have strayed. But to me it's a lesson in wisdom. The younger son comes to the realization that his life was not meant to be that way. He was not meant to be eating pig food. In Jewish tradition, pigs aren't considered of much value; they are even considered unclean. Sitting among the pigs, the prodigal son remembers that even servants in his father's house are beautifully clothed and well fed. But most importantly, he was humble enough to recognize that he was in the wrong and needed to humble himself before his father.

This humility he displays is true wisdom. Though the prodigal son acted rashly throughout the story, his painful realization—that he was wrong and in need of a better life—reveals wisdom at work in his heart. His decision to return to his father's house brings immense joy to his father, fulfilling the truth of Proverbs 23:17—that the father's heart rejoices when his son walks in wisdom.

In contrast, the elder son's pride blinds him. In his self-righteousness, he cannot join the celebration or embrace his brother.

Sometimes wisdom looks like accepting your mistake and apologizing. It may look like respecting and honoring your parents even when you don't want to. It may look like spending time with your younger siblings or teaching them something that you learned. Wisdom is humility. Wisdom is in giving yourself for others.

"Let no one despise your youth but be an example to other believers in the word, in conduct, in love, in spirit, in faith, in purity." (1 Timothy 4:12, NKJV)

Age is usually equated with wisdom. Even in our churches, an older person is considered to be wise. Paul, however, has a different point of view. He wants young Timothy to show wisdom in every aspect of his character so that none of the people in his church would look down upon him or consider him less then.

Your age does not matter to God. If and when He calls you, He is the one who will qualify you. But it is up to you to learn and gain wisdom. Make your conduct such that you gain a reputation as someone who is blessed with wisdom regardless of your age, so that no one can look down on you. Let Holy Spirit be your guide and wisdom be your torch, as you navigate through life.

Paul's encouragement is not only for Timothy but also for us and all young people who love to serve God. Living by the Word and aligning your conduct and character with Scripture prevents others from despising you because of your age. It is clear that being young in age should not be a hindrance as you journey with God. God gives freely when we ask Him for something. As we saw earlier, he gives wisdom without finding fault in us.

And the best way to access God's infinite wisdom is by asking.

I don't know about you, but it sounds like pretty great deal if you ask me.

PRACTICAL KEYS

1. Be in the Word and spend more time with the Lord.

   Search His heart and His will for your life so that your desires are aligned with His.
   Ask Holy Spirit to be your guide.

2. Ask God for wisdom in every aspect of your life.

3. Ask God to help you choose the right company and to make the right decisions that glorify Him in your life.

REFLECTIONS

1. Do you consider yourself a wise woman? If yes, why? If not, why?

2. Have you ever asked God for wisdom?
   Did God answer your prayer?

3. What is your takeaway from this chapter?

5

Pursuing God

"Oh God, you are my God; earnestly I seek you; my soul thirsts for you; my flesh faints for you, as in a dry and weary land where there is no water."
(Psalm 63:1, ESV)

Seeking God is a lifelong pursuit. It is not possible to pursue Him just one day of the week or one week of a year. It is an ongoing pursuit that those who love God and have a desire to know Him choose to do. Pursuing God is not a one-time act, it a lifestyle.

David mastered the art of pursuing God and seeking His face in every circumstance of His life. I love that to him being without God is like living in a barren and dry land. David's soul thirsting for God is one thing, but even his flesh faints for Him. It means that he had trained not just his soul, but also his flesh to seek God. And if he ever felt God was far from him, it even affected his flesh.

How many of us can honestly say this? Can we say that even our flesh yearns for God? I know for sure that my soul yearns for God, but my flesh gets distracted every chance it gets. I am not ashamed to confess that there are days when I clean, cook, watch TV, scroll though my phone and do many other things that may satisfy my flesh rather than spending time with the Lord. I am not proud of it but as Paul has stated, *"The spirit is willing, but the flesh is weak."* (Matthew 26:40-43, NIV)

A life of 'pursuing God' like David requires a lot training and discipline. Which is why we can't choose to seek God just one day a month for 10 minutes and think that it will be enough for our soul and even our flesh. Our flesh needs discipline. It requires a pattern that it can follow. When our soul is in alignment with God, it yearns to be in His presence.

Even Jesus had to take time to converse with the Father in the secret place. In the garden of Gethsemane, He came to check on Peter, John and James twice only to find them sleeping. They were sleeping when they were supposed to keep watch and pray with Jesus. Despite Him being with them and asking them to watch with Him, their flesh was so weak it failed them. As I have said it in a previous chapter, I would not want to be reprimanded by Jesus. I would not be impressed with myself if I found my flesh betraying me in front of Jesus. And if I am honest, it happens more than I would like to admit.

Therefore, I consider the relationship between King David and God something to strive for. David's hunger for God is what makes him a man after God's own heart.

"But seek first the Kingdom of God and His righteousness, and all these things shall be added to you." (Matthew 6:33, NKJV)

David sought the Lord in every circumstance of his life. His pursuit of God never stopped. We never read in the scriptures, "After this, David stopped pursuing the Lord." In fact, the Scriptures make it clear, he praised God even after he lost his son. He sought to bring himself in alignment with God even after the Prophet Nathan told him that he had sinned against the Lord. I can only imagine King Saul throwing a fit and punishing Nathan if he had brought that same message to him. But David honored God's message even though it was not something he would have wanted to hear. Because his pursuit was never earthly. His pursuit was God's heart and God recognized it and called him a *man after his own heart.*

"You will seek me and find me, when you seek me with all your heart."
  (Jeremiah 29:13)

Pursuit of God is rewarded with His presence. Seeking Him with all our heart guarantees He will be found. This is what David understood and practiced. His heart was completely aligned with God when he asked God not to take away His spirit from him - pursuit of God is when there is complete dependence on God's presence.

Making God's presence a priority is what Moses did too. To Moses, it was extremely important that God led them out of Egypt, and he says to God that they would not leave from there without His presence (Exodus 33:15). His vehement refusal to go anywhere without God showed his complete dependence on Him. It reflects how Moses knew that even though he was chosen by God to lead the Israelites out of Egypt, he couldn't do anything without God's presence with them.

We ask God for many things, but we forget to ask for His presence to go with us. We pray for a job and He provides. We pray for exceptional results, and He delivers. We pray for a husband, and He provides. We pray for children and a family of our own, and He provides. He provides all our needs according to His riches and not according to our ability. But more often than not, our pursuit stops here. We get so busy with the blessings that we once asked for that we forget to ask God to come with us.

God made Moses successful when Pharoah agreed to let God's people go. But Moses recognized his need to have God with him on the journey. He didn't just ask God to bless the journey, he asked God to go with them. Now that is what real pursuit looks like.

I would encourage you to not only ask God for His blessings, but His presence. He is the rewarder of those who diligently seek him. If we totally abandon our hearts at His feet and know our need for Him in our lives, He is more than faithful to deliver the promise of His presence.

I have been through catastrophe alone and I have been through catastrophe with Him beside me. And I can guarantee you, it is better to go through trials with Him than without Him. Every single time I have come out unscathed but also more in love with His presence. As I am writing this, tears are welling up, not because of the things I went through but because of God's goodness that went with me in the worst of my times. His goodness was evident in His gentle and comforting presence. And I can testify that I felt Him closer when I was broken and shattered.

God does not lie when He says He can be found when sought. Seek after His presence. Let Him lead you, not just bless you, and let His goodness and mercy follow you. It happens when you desire to pursue Him in every aspect of your life. Over time, we all build something with the Lord. Let us build the Lord as our fortress and shelter like David or let us ask God to be the pillar of fire that goes with us wherever we go.

"The young lions may grow weak and hungry, but those who seek the Lord lack no good thing." (Psalms 34:10)

Our spiritual hunger is always fed by God. Our pursuit of God is rewarded with good things. This scripture gives us assurance of not only God's presence but with it no lack. There will always be good things to satisfy those who pursue the presence of Lord. Just like He promises in Matthew 6:33, that when we prioritize God, He is faithful enough to add everything else to us.

He promises us not only guidance but also provision for our earthly needs. He makes sure that we suffer no lack, whether spiritually or physically. This is not a prosperity Gospel. It is not about bribing God in any way. It is about pursuing God with all our hearts and all our souls. To me there is nothing holier and purer than seeking the face of God and making it a priority all the days of my life.

You may not have an assignment to be a prophet and deliverer like Moses, or a King like David from whose lineage Jesus himself was going to come. You may be a student, or you may have a normal day job. Let yourself be encouraged in this, that seeking God above all else is everyone's calling. Drawing near to Him is for all of us. We don't do it to get something from Him. We seek His face because we know that without God we cannot do anything. Even breathing is a gift from God.

For me, the realization that every breath I take is from Him is enough for me to fall on my face and pursue him. I do not delight in His commands because it is written that I will get the desires of my heart. I delight in His Word because it is life. I delight in His Word because through each word I live.

One cannot seek God without a deep desire to walk in righteousness. Psalms 24:4-6 suggest that those who seek Him have clean hands and pure hearts. Clean hands refer to hands unstained by sin and pure hearts refer to the meek and humble hearts that seek the righteousness of the Lord. Righteousness is the fruit of seeking the Lord. Just as darkness cannot stay in the presence of light, our wholehearted desire to pursue God wipes away all the desire to sin.

In Exodus 33:14, God says to Moses that His presence will bring rest. Relentless pursuit of God has many promises and blessings attached to it, but more than that, it brings His presence. And His presence brings rest.

Moreover, the reason Moses wanted God's presence with them was so that the Israelites could be distinguished from other people. It is so reassuring that God's presence in our lives distinguishes us from others. One of the distinguishing marks of a person who lives in God's presence is rest. This difference between us and others is brought about by our constant pursuit of God. Seeking God and spending time in His word makes us look like Him. Just like Moses' appearance became radiant when he talked to God and it became a marker that he had been in the presence of the Lord, so our lives become a marker that we live in the presence of the Lord.

It is true that His favor rests upon us, but more than that, His presence refines our character. It makes us righteous, bold, generous and humble. It makes us more like Christ. Truth is, when we draw near to God, we accept nothing else and expect nothing less than attributes that glorify Him in us. Every aspect of our lives becomes more aligned with the will of God and we seek to glorify Him through everything we put our mind and hearts to. God's presence with us brings His rest. When we seek His face, He manifests Himself and transforms our hearts and minds. Our way of life and our words become more gracious.

Things that used to satisfy us no longer do - it could be friendships, fame, materialistic pleasures, money or people pleasing that may have satisfied us before, but slowly and steadily our desires become more like Christ as we choose to pursue Him even when our flesh yearns for other things. Suddenly, you come to understand what the psalmist meant by his soul yearning for God like a dear panting for water. Seeking His kingdom changes our priority, and it becomes easier for us to resist the devil. Temptations hold no power over us.

Pursuit of God is simple yet powerful enough to change our lives.

Young women are faced with many ideals of this world - what you must do or look like, what you should eat or how you should look? All these imposed standards of society burden young women to look and talk a certain way, but it is only the pursuit of God that can open their eyes to understand and to prioritize His kingdom. Seeking God renews your mind. Scripture shows you the truth by which to live. And the truth sets you free from all the ideals and idols of the world. Being set free from all the false gods the world wants you to bow down to, you receive blessing and vindication from the Lord himself.

The presence of God is so reassuring and loving that even I, like Moses, want Him to go before me. There was a time when I wanted to move to a different location, but God clearly said to me that even though He won't ever stop me from going anywhere, but He wouldn't be going with me. Needless to say, this Moses moment was enough for me to stay right where I was and wait for the right timing from Him.

I have personally experienced how He makes His will clear to us. And if we are familiar with His voice, we will know if we are aligned with His will or not. It is His pursuit in the secret place that makes us, His sheep, know His voice. This is one of the benefits of our constant pursuit of Him, that we become increasingly accustomed to His voice and His way of dealing with us.

We become familiar with Him as we pursue Him more and more. As we grow closer to Him, we begin to understand why David's soul yearned for His presence or why Daniel prayed three times a day against the will of the king, and why Moses wouldn't go anywhere without God.

> **REFLECTIONS**
>
> 1. Is your pursuit of God a way to get what you desire now, or is it a constant pursuit which makes you more like Christ?
>
> 2. Do you look more like Christ or more like the world?
>
> 3. How has this chapter helped you understand God more?

6

Anxious Thoughts

"Do not be anxious about anything, but in every situation, by prayer and petition, with thanksgiving, present your requests to the Lord." (Philippians 4:6)

According to the Australian government, 18% of Australians were dispensed a mental health related prescription in 2023-24. I don't know about you, but that number seems quite high. These are the people who are currently medicated; there may be many more on waitlists to see specialists and even more who are battling anxiety and depression on a daily basis but are too ashamed to get help or think they do not need any help. With all this in mind, I can only imagine the statistics skyrocketing.

I have had anxiety and even panic attacks. I was close to being diagnosed with postpartum depression. I have personally experienced a mental health crisis. And I have overcome it with the help of God. Now, I am not diminishing the need for medication for certain things that may prevent you functioning in your day-to-day life, but I am of the school of thought that nothing is impossible for our God. I have tasted and seen that He is good.

You may not have anxiety but have anxious thoughts. Thoughts about things going terribly wrong all the time. Maybe you're an overthinker who triggers anxiety by running things through your mind again and again. Whatever category you belong to, know that there is a way out. God is a good God and He has amazing plans for your future.

God knows that the enemy will use our thoughts against us. He will fire his thoughts like arrows towards us, waiting for us to be struck by at least one. Accepting just one such anxiety inducing thought - which is a lie, will make us run in circles for days on end. Initially, it may not look like you need to surrender the thought or cancel it in the name of Jesus. It may just look like your own thought because our brains have an amazing ability to justify everything it thinks. You may also have justified why you think you will, for example, never be able to get that job, or get good grades, or make to your school football team. These thoughts might not seem serious on the surface, but once you accept them as your own and meditate on them, they can become an issue or even a reason for anxiety.

Our brain has a powerful neural network called RAS, reticular activating system. It is responsible for activating our consciousness, arousal and focused attention. When we think a thought enough times, this neural network functions to bring the particulars of our thought to our attention by activating focused attention. For example, when you're on the road and see a yellow car, you then begin to see many yellow cars. This happens when RAS gets activated and your brain focuses on all the yellow cars. This gives you the illusion that there is a sudden increase in the number of yellow cars on the road. The enemy knows what he is doing when he throws negative or anxiety inducing thoughts at us. When we choose to focus on certain thoughts, our brain begins working to prove them true, highlighting evidence from our lives that supports them — and in doing so, keeps us trapped within those very thoughts. You must have heard the saying that we attract what we think about. It is this neural network that functions in overdrive making us believe that by thinking a thought we attract what we are thinking about. But the reality is, the evidence of it is just more visible to us because we are focusing on it. Like the yellow cars – in reality there weren't more on the road, we were just noticing them by changing our focus. Flipping this concept, positive thoughts may highlight an opportunity which otherwise might not have been visible to us.

It may not always be possible to present everything to God at the exact moment it is happening. But once you recognize that the thought doesn't glorify God in any way, then it is imperative to give it to the Lord. God knows how the enemy can induce worries in our minds, and so He has given us scriptures to use against them. He asks us to cast all our cares upon Him. He asks us not to worry, but in prayer give everything to the Lord.

God has given us a way to bring our worries to His feet - He wants us to do it with thanksgiving. A thankful and grateful heart cannot be overwhelmed by worry. It is impossible to worry when your heart is filled with gratitude. He wants us to remember all the good things and be thankful for them and give all our troubles to Him. This is so that we remember His goodness which He showed us in the past and put our worrying thoughts in His hands knowing we can trust in His wisdom and goodness. This again engages our RAS to focus on and highlight only the positives in our life. I absolutely love how the Lord has laid it down like a strategy for us to use as weapon.

Psalm 100:4 states that we need to enter His gates with thanksgiving and His courts with praise. In order to submit a petition to the Lord and lay it all down before Him, we should enter with praise and thanksgiving. Thanksgiving opens the gates to the Lord so that we can approach Him with all our cares and anxious thoughts.

So, next time you have a thought that, for example, you're not going to get the job you want, go into your secret place and remind your heart about all the times God has come through. Think about all the history you've made with God and praise His name that because He has done it before He can do it again.

"Therefore, do not worry about tomorrow, for tomorrow will worry about itself. Each day has enough trouble of its own." (Matthew 6:34)

I have come to realize over the years that worrying is a form of self-reliance. We are called to be dependent on God. The Bible asks us not to lean not on our own understanding. But what worry really does is, within the limits of our own understanding, it creates the illusion that we can somehow change our situation or navigate the storm on our own. It convinces us that we are alone—that it all depends on us. And when that thought takes hold, we run with it. Instead of surrendering our circumstances to the Lord, we begin to glorify them instead of glorifying Him in our situation.

So, by worrying we really are trusting in our own ability to handle a situation rather than the infinite wisdom of God. We cannot change anything by worrying, and so Jesus wisely asks us not to worry about tomorrow.

In Matthew 6:32, Jesus says that God already knows our needs. He knows what we need and when we need it. He wants us to posture our hearts towards His Kingdom, which is imperishable, rather than worry about eating and drinking which is perishable. God, in all His goodness provides for all our needs – His name is Jehovah Jireh. Provider is His name and also His character and God never behaves out of character. He stays true to Himself.

Jesus asks whether we can increase or decrease the length of our life by being anxious. Can we change someone else's perception of us by worrying? Can we gain anything, but fear, by being anxious? Therefore, it is foolish to worry about things that are beyond our control. Focusing our energy on worrying is beneficial to no one.

Moreover, anxious thoughts arise because of fear. It could be the fear of rejection or fear of failure. My nationality is Indian, and societal pressure to succeed is intense. Therefore, I have struggled with fear of failure most of my life. The only thing I can say with certainty is that Lord does not look at our achievements. This was something my spiritual mentor told me.

God's measure of success is the posture of our hearts. God was not impressed by all the battles King Saul had won for Israel. He certainly wasn't impressed by how well-built David's brothers were. He did not even consider their impressive resume which included fighting for their national army on the frontlines. All He considered was the devotion of the heart, which He found in David. God does not see what and how men see. I have found comfort in this, and I can assure you, if you surrender your thoughts to God, you will find rest in this knowledge too.

I am grateful to God, that He cares enough to look at my heart and not just at my achievements, for which I may have nothing to show.

Proverbs 21:31 says, *"The horse is made ready for the day of battle but victory rests with the Lord."* I believe that not being anxious about tomorrow is wisdom. Anxious thoughts are habitual and so our brain needs training to reject them every time they occur. Equipping ourselves with Scripture and wearing the full armor of God is what becomes our defense against these tactics of the enemy.

"Finally, brothers and sisters, whatever is true, whatever is noble, whatever is right, whatever is pure, whatever is lovely, whatever is admirable - if anything is excellent or praiseworthy- think about such things." (Philippians 4:8)

Paul wrote this letter to the Philippians while he was in prison. The Christinas in Philippi were suffering a great deal because of the Gospel, but Paul urges them to be bold and to spread the Gospel that Jesus Christ is the Lord. But, even in suffering he asks them to be joyful and think about the things that are true, pure and lovely. He is asking them to set their focus on what the good news really means. He is surely speaking from experience. After all, he is writing this from prison.

When Paul and Silas began to worship in the prion, the gates opened (Acts 16:16-40). All their physical bondages were broken. Because they were thinking about what was excellent and praiseworthy. They were not only focusing on what was praiseworthy but praising the One who is praiseworthy. In his letter to the Philippians, Paul preached what he had experienced. If we want to be free from fear and anxiety, let's think about the things that are good and pure. Focus on Jesus.

Paul also writes in the letter to the Romans about the importance of renewing and transforming one's mind. Paul was a missionary and had been to prison many times and I can only guess at the assault of the enemy on his mind. It can't be easy to encourage others while in prison, but Paul managed to do it. He had laid his fear and anxiety at the feet of Jesus. We can see this when he says that for him to live is Christ and die is gain. He has learnt to be content in whatever circumstances God allows.

This is faith in the goodness of God. There was no anxiety worrying about his future. There is no fear of failure or of rejection. When he was been rejected by the people who rejected Christ, he didn't let that settle in his mind. His focus was on what was good, pure, and lovely.

"Casting down imaginations and every high thing that exalts itself against the knowledge of God and bringing into captivity every thought to the obedience of Christ." (2 Corinthians 10:5, NKJV)

This is one of my go-to verses when I battle with anxious or negative thoughts. Paul encourages us to cast down imaginations - he calls our fears and anxiety vain imaginations. They are nothing but lofty images our mind produces to keep us prisoners of fear. Any thought that challenges our knowledge of God must be brought into obedience to Jesus. When we are scared of failure, we do not believe in God's ability to work everything out for our good. Our fear tries to rise above the goodness of God, so it must be taken captive. Every thought that we do not take captive takes us captive.

It is a plan of the enemy to keep us locked in the cycle of anxious thoughts so that they imprison us. His plan is that we never rise above our fears and so never enter the destiny God has for us.

I want to remind you that when we are born again, we are given the mind of Christ and we do hold the thoughts of His heart (1 Corinthians 2:16, AMPC). When we are born again, old things have passed away, and all things have become new (2 Corinthians 5:17). The more we surrender our lives to God, the more old cycles of fear and anxiety are broken as all things are made new. When we hold the thoughts of Christ in our minds, there is no place for any lofty imaginations to take hold.

"In this world you will have trouble. But take heart! I have overcome the world." (John 16:33)

Jesus does not say that things will be easy. In fact, He says that we will have troubles of many kinds in this world. We may have physical ailments or mental ailments. We may experience betrayal in relationships and friendships. We may not get the desires of our hearts. We might not have food on our tables or shelter over our heads. But Jesus still encourages us to let our hearts rest in the fact that He has overcome the world. He wants us to rest in the fact that He is an almighty God who works everything out for our good.

God is faithful and good to keep us in His care in any circumstance. Instead of letting anxious thoughts rule our minds, approaching God for His grace and mercy is what makes the enemy lose his foothold in our minds. Jesus empathizes with us and does not look down upon us or condemn us. In fact, He wants all our anxious thoughts brought to Him. What a gracious God!

REFLECTIONS

1. What is an anxiety inducing thought you struggle with the most? Look for a scripture which is opposite to what your anxiety is. Meditate on it. Write it on a sticky note and stick it on your bedside table. Speak it out every morning.

For example: If you worry about losing a job or that you may not have enough for yourself, you can meditate on how God values even little sparrows and provides for them
(Matt 6:26-30). Write on a sticky note, "I am valuable to God and He provides for me." (Write in the present tense and not past tense).

2. What is one thing that you're grateful for?

3. How has this chapter helped make you more aware of your thought life?
Do you now feel equipped to tackle unwanted thoughts?

7

Joy

"The prospect of the righteous is joy." (Proverbs 10:28)

In this world, people often chase happiness. Happiness is an emotion, and just like any other emotion it is contingent upon our circumstances. Moreover, happiness is fleeting. It lasts only for a finite amount of time. Happiness is often related to worldly pleasures which people spend their life pursuing. It is not a bad emotion. It just isn't long-lasting.

Joy, however, comes from the inside. It does not depend on our circumstances. It does not require us to chase worldly, fleeting pleasures. It is not materialistic. A one-time dopamine hit cannot produce eternal joy. Joy is a fruit of Spirit. Being filled with Holy Spirit is what produces joy. 1 Peter 1:9 states that believing in Jesus is what fills us with inexpressible and glorious joy.

I know it may seem naive or simply gullible, but in my younger years I did not know the difference between happiness and joy. I used to run after all the pleasures that the world had to offer. I followed whatever new fad the world followed at that time. I was simply looking for validation from friends. I am not proud of being naive, but in my defense,

I never had anyone teach me the difference between joy and happiness. So, I began searching for it where everyone else was looking.

I did not understand that believing in Jesus and being filled with the Holy Spirit is what produces joy. The prospect of the righteous is joy. Righteous ones are the ones who can anticipate joy. The question I often ask myself is whether I knew what joy was. And if I am honest, I did not. I am in no way insinuating that if anyone is chasing worldly happiness, they are not familiar with the joy of the Lord. Being filled with joy is what produces happiness. Happiness is the byproduct of a joyful heart.

"Rejoice always, pray continually, give thanks in all circumstances; for it is God's will for you in Christ Jesus." (1 Thessalonians 5:16-18)

Paul urges the believers to rejoice always. Whatever their circumstances, he asks them to always rejoice, regardless. It is God's will for us to rejoice in Christ Jesus. God's desire for us is to be joyful. To be filled with the infinite joy that comes only through our Savior Jesus.

I can only imagine this is supernatural joy. Because anything of this world is limited, fleeting and superficial. But anything that comes from above is perfect. Just like the salvation we have received is perfect, so is the joy that comes with it.

Joy is a state of mind rather than an emotion. It is mastered when we learn to rest in Jesus. When we understand that no matter what our lives look like at the moment, God holds us up in His righteous right hand. At the moment, it may seem that joy is not an option for you. It may seem that God is too far away to even see what may be going on. It may seem impossible to feel joy. But Paul asks us to, *"Consider it pure joy, my brothers and sisters, whenever you face trials of many kinds, because you know that the testing of your faith produces perseverance."* (James 1:2-4).

Paul doesn't ask us to feel joy. He is asking us to consider it as joy. When we are suffering, we remember that even Jesus suffered while He lived on Earth, and we are sharing in His suffering. Therefore, consider it a joy to be sharing in what Jesus went through.

Our troubles may be different to what Jesus went through in His lifetime. Our troubles may be loneliness, heartbreaks, failures, rejection or slander. But rest in the thought that Jesus went through all kinds of temptations in the face of challenges. Before considering vengeance or unforgiveness, let us consider being joyful. For me it was a long and tough road to follow this scripture. Without God's help the very first thing which comes out of us in the face of trials is sin. But we have a choice – to follow our sinful nature or follow the Spirit. It takes the power of the Holy Spirit and our willingness to make our sinful nature be obedient to the word of God that helps us resist temptation.

"You make me known the path of life; you will fill me with joy in your presence, with eternal pleasures at your right hand." (Psalm 16:11)

God is the giver of joy. It is His attribute which is given to us by His grace when we believe in His son and receive the Holy Spirit. Zephaniah 3:17 states that God rejoices over us with singing. He is the one who rejoices in us and is glad in us and hence we become joyful in Him. There is no other source of joy but God. It is in His presence that we are filled with eternal joy.

Our culture shows us many different ways to be happy. It has mastered ways to give us a dopamine hit that makes us feel momentary pleasure. Ironically, the number of people taking anti-depressants is on the rise. Depression, just like anxiety, in on the rise. If people are constantly seeking happiness and are following whatever their hearts desire, then it follows that the rates of depression and anxiety should decrease.

The only way to fill one's heart with joy is through Jesus. The worldly pleasures are momentary, but eternal pleasures are at God's right hand. It is the presence of God that fills our hearts with joy, eternal joy. So, when Paul asks us to rejoice always his desire for us is to be in the presence of the Lord. His presence can break any depressive bondage over our minds. The reason why Paul and Silas were able to worship even while in prison was because of this joy that filled their hearts. The joy that makes us sing comes from the one who rejoices and sings over us.

"Joy of the Lord is your strength." (Nehemiah 8:10)

There may be ample reason for us to grieve. We may be in the middle of a storm and the only thing we can see is the storm. When the storm that is brewing outside begins to take shape inside us, we must seek refuge in the presence of the Lord. That is the source of joy. Hope in the Lord is what gives us strength to bear all. Knowing that our Savior is with us and empathizes with us makes it easier to stand and not fall in all the challenges we face in this world.

Sometimes our joy becomes strength for others too. Sharing the hope we have even in affliction allows us to bring the joy of salvation to those around us. When Peter and John were asked for money from a paralyzed man, they responded saying they did not have gold or silver, but they were willing to give whatever they had. And what they had was the power of the Holy Spirit which made the paralyzed man walk. Similarly, we can share joy, which is a fruit of the Spirit, with others.

The psalmist talks about the oil of joy. He says that God has anointed him with the oil of joy and has set him above his companions. He understood what Paul wrote - to consider it all joy. Not only does joy enable us to stand in the face of a trial, with strength, but it sets us above our companions. Because, when your companions are complaining and losing hope, you're filled with joy because of the knowledge that you're partaking in suffering with Jesus.

Moreover, in John 16:24, Jesus encourages us to ask for anything in His name, and we will receive it so that our joy may be complete. He is assuring His disciples that in His name and through His name our joy can be full.

A cheerful heart is like good medicine and therefore a heart filled with joy helps us go through our troubles.

Paul talks about his trials in 2 Corinthians 6. He talks about all his hardships, including beatings, prison, dishonor and being betrayed. He states that even though he is sorrowful, he is always rejoicing because even though he has nothing he possesses everything in Christ Jesus. Having everlasting joy doesn't mean there won't be any troubles or that we will be shielded from it, because joy doesn't depend on outside circumstances. If it did it wouldn't be eternal.

God is not asking us to be unaffected by what is going on in our lives. Instead, He wants us to trust Him in the brewing storm. Joy becomes evident when we know that being in His presence is the only thing we need.

> ### REFLECTIONS
>
> 1. What do you think is the difference between joy and happiness? Have you experienced both or one before?
>
> 2. If there ever was a time when God has come through as your joy, even in your suffering, remember it. Write it down.

8

Waiting

"Therefore, the Lord awaits to be gracious to you, and therefore he exalts himself to show mercy to you. For the Lord is the God of justice; blessed are all those who wait for him." (Isaiah 30:18, NKJV)

In the course of this lifetime, we go through many seasons. Each season produces certain fruit in us. Waiting is also a season that we go through many times in life. It is a season where our patience and faith are tested, and the fruit of endurance is produced. The Lord never wastes any season. He uses each and every season to build us to be more like Him so that we may become the aroma of Christ in the world.

Isaiah 30:18 states that the Lord awaits to be gracious to us. God waits for us to turn to Him so that He can show His grace to us. Patience is an attribute of His that is produced within us in the season of waiting. God gave us His only Son and still waits for us to turn to Him. His heart is for us to experience His unending love and mercy.

God prepares us in the waiting so that we can see His glory. Sometimes our season of waiting is simply to bring us closer to Him so that we may know Him better. My journey of waiting could initially have been summed up in one sentence. It was a journey from, "I only have God" to, "I only need God." And I still stand by this. Every time I get frustrated in the waiting, I remind myself that God is the only one I need. Whether it be for the journey of waiting or something beyond.

I have always noticed that in the waiting, God is silent. He is around us, but He wants us to look for Him. Just like the scripture states, He exalts Himself so that He can show us mercy. He doesn't hide, He is just at a higher altitude than us (metaphorically speaking), so He wants us to climb to meet Him. So that we can experience His grace and mercy.

Before the birth of Jesus, God was silent for four hundred years. His silence didn't mean He wasn't present. He exalted Himself so that He could show His love and mercy through Jesus. And then we see His amazing grace. In fact, we get to experience it every single day. The salvation that came after the period of waiting, is what brought us, not only closer to God, but it brought us a Mediator who stood between us and God who still intercedes for us.

After the ascension of Jesus Christ, the disciples waited for fifty days and then were filled with the Holy Spirit. Again, after a season of waiting, we are always filled with more of God. We experience more of Him and grow closer to Him so that we may fulfill whatever God has planned for us in our next season.

Our season of waiting can also be the time the enemy uses to tempt us in every way. The Biblical account which sheds light on this is when Moses went up the mountain to speak to God and returned after ten days. The Israelites grew so impatient that they thought Moses was dead and elected Aaron to be their priest and asked him to make a golden calf with all the gold they had. Upon Moses' return, he was horrified by the sight of the Israelites worshiping a god they had made.

It is insane to me that even though they had experienced God's goodness for so long and in every way - He brought them out of Egypt, killed Pharaoh and destroyed his armies, went with them as a pillar of fire and protected them and he gave them manna to eat. But during the waiting they became prey to temptation. Maybe Aaron was doubtful too or maybe he just wanted to please the people so they wouldn't be difficult to lead because he had seen Moses struggle. The reasons could be many, but the ten days of waiting was enough for them to fall into temptation. And three thousand people lost their lives in the judgement that followed.

We may not be so severely judged for our slip-ups and will be forgiven if we get tempted during our waiting season, but giving in to temptation is something we have to avoid. As the Scripture says, God is working inside of us during the waiting. He wants us to experience His grace and therefore He allows us to think that He is far from us so that we will look for Him. We may seek His face in the secret place. He wants us to worship Him so that He can grow our roots deeper into him.

"But those who wait on the Lord shall renew their strength; they shall mount up with wings like eagles; they shall run and not be weary; they shall walk and not faint." (Isaiah 40:31, NKJV)

An eagle can sense when a storm is brewing. It waits for the storm on the high plains and while it waits, it keeps its eyes on the heights above. As soon as the storm breaks, the eagle flies into the storm and uses it to reach greater heights while other birds are hiding. This is how the eagle mounts up using strategic flight inside the storm while keeping its focus on where it wants to get to. Similarly, this is how the supernatural strength is renewed in the life of a believer - by keeping their eyes on the Lord whether in the season of waiting or going through a storm.

It is wise to believe that God's plans are higher than ours even when it seems like there is nothing happening. God uses storms to lift us higher and draw us near to Him.

"And let us not grow weary while doing good, for in due season we shall reap, if we do not lose heart." (Galatians 6:9, NKJV)

Waiting is not necessarily a period when God calls us to do nothing. He may ask us to be watchful or maybe volunteer at our church, or He may ask us to tell someone the Good News of the Gospel. God can ask us to share our testimony. In the waiting period our obedience can be tested. God can ask us to use our giftings to serve His kingdom or He may ask us to simply seek Him. As the scripture states, at the end of waiting season and in due time, we will receive the fruit. God does not forget the promise He has made. When we wait on the Lord and don't give up, we reap a harvest in due season.

Years ago, I was alone in the United States of America. I went there to study, but during the summer vacation I did not have a place to stay. So, I got in touch with an old connection of mine and she got me a place to live for a period of three months. I did not have any money and didn't know anyone, but I still went. I could not find any work/internship there. Moreover, the roommates I had were not good to me. They used to laugh at me behind my back and used very harsh words to describe me while I was not in the room. I was given a bathroom for showering which had a faulty drainage system. They didn't have a washer, so I had to wash my clothes in the bathroom where the water never drained, so my clothes had a horrible stench to them.

I have not even scratched the surface of the hate I received from them. Overall, I was in a sticky situation. I had just come back to God the previous semester and had begun to understand the goodness of God, but this experience was like coming face-to-face with a storm. Then the Lord prompted me to talk to one of my friends to ask her if I could stay with her and her husband. I had known them for just four months prior to asking this huge favor. She was also pregnant. I knew I was taking a chance and would have been okay if her reply was negative. Instead, she said that the Lord had given her Galatians 6:9 that day and so she knew God was asking something from of her.

She was okay with me staying with her even though she was facing her own struggles. And I tried as best I could not to be any trouble. I am eternally grateful to both of them. When I think back to this time, I was definitely blessed spiritually by both of them, but God also blessed them with a brand-new home and a healthy baby immediately after they did what God asked them to do.

The whole situation will stay with me my whole life - people who showed me kindness during their waiting season, and God, who did not leave me in the storm. God's ways will always be higher and better. I am what I am right now because of the help of many such people that God used to bless me, whether I was in waiting or in a new season. I am sure they reaped amazing fruit out of their obedience to God.

God can use the season of waiting as a season of learning, but at the same time, if we are not rooted in the Word, we can easily lose focus and resort to complaining and whining. And as the Scripture says, we reap what we sow. Whining does not glorify God and thus produces no fruit, or even rotten fruit. I have learnt to keep my eyes on the Lord rather than on what is happening around me so as to not grumble and get lost in the waiting and never understanding the higher plans of God.

"But as for me, I will look to the lord; I will wait for the God of my salvation, My God will hear me." (Micah 7:7, ESV)

The name of Jesus, Emmanuel, means "God with us." Whenever we go through waiting periods when God is silent, it is imperative for us to believe He is with us. Knowing this not only helps us navigate the rough path with confidence but also helps us to keep our eyes on Him, to set our focus on him. Scripture says that without knowledge we perish. Without the knowledge and the awareness of God's presence with us, we are likely to react in an ungodly manner or take an unholy path or turn to the world for solace, thereby creating distance between ourselves and the Lord.

God promised Abraham that he would be the father of nations. But, while he waited for Isaac, Abram had Ishmael who later became, and still is, a taunting figure to Isaac. You may be waiting for your Isaac, as in something the Lord has promised, or you may simply be waiting for an answer from God. And it may be easier to insert yourself and your own understanding into God's plan, but trying to produce results using our own wisdom will produce rotten fruit.

Keeping our eyes on God and trusting His plans for us is what gets us through the season of waiting and positions us to receive all that God has for us. To me this sounds like a better plan. I don't have to do anything but just wait on the Lord. Waiting is not wasted; it produces endurance within us. It builds our character and renews our strength.

The scripture in Micah states that in our waiting, God hears us. This is the assurance that even though God seems to be far away, His ears still hear our cries and our prayers.

"For the revelation awaits an appointed time; it speaks of the end and will not prove false. Though it linger, wait for it; it will certainly come and will not delay." (Habakkuk 2:3)

When the Lord speaks a promise to us, He has already appointed a time for it. He knows how much time the vision will wait in order for us to produce the fruit He desires. To us, it may look like it is lingering and that it may not come. We may begin to lose hope, but the only thing required of us during this time is to wait for it to come to pass. Because nothing God has spoken will return void or be delayed. Trusting in God is what helps us keep our eyes on Him.

Every promise already has an appointed time and future. All the visions we have received come with a date. We may think God is delaying answering a prayer or fulfilling a promise, but He never delays. Just as the sun knows the time to rise and set and does so daily without fail, our vision knows the time to come to pass.

This is encouraging for me. His wisdom is trustworthy, and His understanding is far beyond my reach. Just waiting on Him and resting in this thought that He holds every aspect of my future, whether I know it or not, brings me peace and security.

One thing I have always done and still do, is sit with God and process everything happening or not happening around me. It helps me stay away from frustration in the season of waiting. It helps me not complain too much and keeps my heart and thoughts tethered in the One who I know - the One who holds my future in His hands.

REFLECTIONS

1. Do you know what season you're in? Journal your emotions as well as your prayer life. Write down what is happening around you in your relationships and friendships. Does God feel close or far from you?

2. Has the Lord given you any vision for the future? If so, write it down and make it clear just like God asked Habakkuk to make it plain in writing. Pray through it and
war* for the vision every day in your secret place.

*For a Christian, we always war on our knees. Claim every promise in prayer that the Lord has given you. Back it with the Scripture.

Believing what the Lord says and not putting a limitation on yourself is another form of war. It is a war against a limited mindset. Pray for faith.

Pray Ephesians 3:20 and repeat it to exercise your 'belief' muscle.

Receiving is another war. Practice gratefulness to counter this. Thank God for everything He has done for you and given you in your daily life.

9

Obedience

"Now this is love: that we walk in obedience to his commands. As you have heard from the beginning, his command is that you walk in love."
(2 John 1:6)

In the culture I come from, obedience is demanded and so is respect for those in authority and our elders. Consequently, I have not struggled much with following commands or being obedient or doing what I am told. Of course I have had my rebellious phase, just like any other teenager, but I quickly went back to my roots. Unfortunately though, because of this culture of obedience which is ingrained in children from an early age, there are authority figures and elders who misuse their positions. I have been in workplaces where employees were insulted by employers using foul language. I have seen elders abusing their authority, while young people are expected to tolerate everything in the name of respect.

But the scripture above teaches us that to obey means to love. Love is what creates obedience, not the weight of false expectations imposed by those above us because of position or age. It may seem counter intuitive, but it makes sense. Because God's love gives you freedom so that you want to obey Him. Not out of fear but out of freedom. The word 'obedience' may seem harsh, as we so often associate it with fear. As a result, we see God as a hard taskmaster when it comes to obedience. But the opposite is true.

Out of His love for us, God gave His one and only Son. And Jesus, out of His love for His father, gave away His life. What a beautiful picture of obedience! God emptied himself first so that we may receive eternal life with Him and in turn we are to love Him and believe in Him. And His love language is obedience. Obedience to His standards. Obedience to the laws that are written on our hearts.

God has already modeled that perfect obedience is through love. Hence, if anyone presents another model of obedience, it is unbiblical. That was what was wrong with the cultural model that I followed and had to unlearn. Love is what creates respect and obedience, not the other way round. We walk in His commands out of our love for Him, and His command is to walk in love. If this isn't poetic, I don't know what is.

"He replied, 'Blessed are those who hear the word of God and obey it.'" (Luke 11:28)

The consequence of obedience is blessing from the Lord. And disobedience has its consequences too. If obedience makes us like Christ, disobedience takes us away from Christ. Disobedience to the commands of God is nothing more than sin. And the consequence of sin is death. Now, it is up to us whether we choose blessing or death.

Whatever we choose has eternal consequences for us. But it also has consequences for our future generations. Just as Eve's disobedience caused both her and Adam to be separated from God — a consequence that impacted her — sin then found an opening in their generational line, and their son Cain became the first murderer. Our choices are reflected in our children and our children's children. Which is why it says in Proverbs that a wise man leaves an inheritance for his children's children. This inheritance is not just monetary, it is also the consequences of either obedience or disobedience. Making the correct choice is up to us.

It is better to obey God than to obey men. Even Peter said that when he was standing in front of the court. When we think God wants us to obey people at all times, no matter what, this type of thinking can keep us in bondage in ungodly relationships. There are many young women who think they cannot leave their toxic parents or marital relationships with in-laws or even husbands, thinking that they are being obedient to God. But what they are doing is being obedient to the command that God gave without understanding that obedience is born out of love. Obedience comes as a result of love for God and love for people. Asking for obedience should not be to control people, but out of love for them. God's love for us never demands obedience from us when that 'obedience' causes us harm.

If you don't take anything from this chapter, take this - that love is what brings freedom and out of that freedom we obey. Obey not because it is commanded, rather obey because of love. The relationships that command obedience must first give love freely. I recommend every young woman must test their relationships, whether in romantic relationships, friendships or familial relationships.

"For this is the love for God, that we keep His commandments. And His commandments are not burdensome." (1 John 5:3, ESV)

Keeping God's commands are not burdensome when they are done out of love for Him. We love because He first loved us and showed us love by giving away Himself as a sacrifice so that we could be reconciled to the Father. When we understand the word of God, that His sacrifice is because of His love for us, we do everything out of love for Him.

All the apostles waited for the Holy Spirit to come upon them, just as Jesus asked them. Then they went on to fulfill the great commission as commanded by Jesus. These things were not burdensome to them. They did it out of love and out of belief that Jesus is the Messiah. Where there is unbelief, there is no love and thus following the commands of God become burdensome.

The Israelites were caught in the sin of unbelief too, which was the reason for all their grumbling and complaining against God. They made everything hard for themselves by simply not believing. They saw the hand of God in every situation but still chose to live in unbelief. Consequently, being obedient to God became a burden to them.

I have experienced a similar thing. Whenever God wants me to leave particular place, He takes away my love for that place. Consequently, everything around me feels like a burden and I want to get out of there and move as soon as possible. This is definitely a way God communicates with me.

In our lives too, it is easier to be obedient to our parents when we do it out of love. If, however, we discover we are being pressurized into doing something, we have this innate knowing that love does not come with any kind of pressure. So, when we love God with all our heart, mind, and strength, it is easier for us to follow His commands. It is easier for us to show love to our neighbors and kindness to our enemies. Walking in obedience to the Lord becomes our second nature.

Moreover, we know that God's commands are *for* us, so that we may be able to live a full life with Him. His moral laws are *for* us. Currently, knowing right from wrong is not fashionable, but this knowledge is what keeps us on the path of our destiny that God has kept for us. Going against the command of the Lord led Adam and Eve to lose the close relationship they had with God.

Disobedience creates a gap between us and God. The enemy uses shame to keep us away from God. And when we know that we have compromised on God's moral standard, we feel it becomes harder for us to face Him, further deepening the gap between us and God. Shame becomes a bondage and love slowly begins to vanish. Disobedience becomes easier when obedience seems out of reach. It seems like a burden. Just like Adam and Eve, our blessing is taken away. Being in God's presence is a blessing.

2 Corinthians 10:5 states that we have to bring even our thoughts into obedience to Christ. Even our thought-lives need to be submitted to the Lord. It becomes second nature when we understand that obedience is for our good - so that we may not lose our intimate relationship with the Lord.

"As obedient children, do not conform to the evil desires you had when you lived in ignorance." (1 Peter 1:14)

The desire to be disobedient is attributed to our old self. But as we come to believe in Jesus as our Savior, our desires imitate His desires. This is what Paul meant when he said, *"Imitate me, just as I imitate Christ."* (I Corinthians 11:1, AMP) When we put our faith in Christ, our desires align with that of Jesus as He becomes alive within us. Hence, it becomes almost impossible for us to fulfill the evil desires that we had as a sinner. But we need to bring all that to the feet of Jesus in order to fully walk in obedience.

God is so faithful to us that even when all we want to do is stay away from Him, He not only pursues us, but sees it simply as ignorance when we choose the world over Him. For our evil desires – those desires that satisfy our flesh and bring us fleeting happiness for a couple of days, are nothing more than a sign of ignorance. When we come into the knowledge of Him, we become more like Him, led by the Spirit who brings us closer to God.

When I was young, I did not know that I had to be obedient to God. Looking back, I think it's funny that I thought my dad was the one who made all these rules – don't date anyone, go to church every week, wear modest clothes, walk in purity etc. Needless to say, I did not understand a single one of these rules because there was no explanation or even clarity about what they meant. These rules were a burden to me, and I did rebel in my own way. For a while, I strayed when I went to a different city to study. I thought that inter-faith dating was okay because I wasn't told why it was not up to the standard of God. For me it was just a set of rules that my father had asked me to follow.

It was not until much later in my life that God showed Himself to me through His Word and I became obsessed with following Christ. I fell in love with God and His Word, and that is how I began following His commands.

Maybe you are also told to follow certain rules, even when you don't understand the real reason behind them. I encourage you to read the Word and ask Holy Spirit to reveal Jesus to you and to make every word real. Then you will have a revelation of Christ within you which is the hope of glory.

Even though it will be tough, the love of God will make it easier for you to obey God rather than disobeying Him.

When I tell my daughter to do something, I can often see the unwillingness to obey on her face. She takes her time to think and decide whether she wants to do as I say or not. Sometimes she does it and sometimes she doesn't. More often than not, she chooses to disobey. Rebellion and defiance are what we are born with and don't need to be taught. Obedience needs to be taught. It takes discipline, discipleship, good values and morals. It takes patience and love for God to walk in obedience every day. All I know is that it isn't easy, but it is worth it.

Walking in obedience to God has brought me so much joy and peace. Sometimes what God asks us to do doesn't make sense to us at the time, or to others. And truth be told, it doesn't have to make sense in the moment. Obedience often reflects our faith - whether we are faithful, even when we don't understand. Abraham was obedient to the point that he was ready to sacrifice his son, for whom he had waited for years. He was able to take Isaac to the mount to sacrifice him, because he had faith in God. He knew the goodness of God. He knew God is faithful no matter what. Abraham didn't hold anything back from Him and thus he is called the father of all nations.

Faith comes when we set our eyes on Jesus and keep His word in our hearts. Being in the secret place with Him and hiding the Word in our hearts is what familiarizes us with His character and His goodness. Our faith is often tested in troubles and trials but as it becomes stronger, so does our willingness to be obedient. Faith is what makes us obedient to God.

"Do not merely do listen to the word and so deceive yourselves. Do what it says." (James 1:22)

We are hypocrites if we do not do what the Word says. James states that we deceive ourselves when we aren't obedient. Jesus called pharisees and teachers of the law hypocrites. They were the ones who had made their lives all about following the Scriptures. But the problem was that their lives were all about rules and rituals. Their obedience lacked love for God. For them, following the rules was much more important than loving God. Consequently, they did not recognize Him when God Himself walked in midst of them.

Obedience is better than sacrifice.

Sometimes God asks us to do something, like for example, a gentle nudge to talk to someone about him, or share your lunch/meal with someone who is sad or lonely, or He may want you to share the Good News with someone. Once, God asked me to pray for someone while I was working a summer job cleaning dorms in my university. It took me more than three days, but eventually I got up the courage to pray for that person. She had a pain in her ankle and often had to sit while working. Guess what, I prayed for her and asked God to heal her. Even though He wanted me to pray for her, and I did, she did not get healed. But she was grateful for the prayer. The next day she was in less pain, and I counted that as a little victory.

What was God teaching me? He didn't completely heal her. At the time, I didn't know why my prayer didn't result in a miracle for that girl. But the more I sit with this memory, the more I realize it was not about healing, It was about obedience. God wanted to see if I would do what He wanted me to do. And I have always done what God asks me to do. Sometimes at the expense of my self-respect. And sometimes against the advice of the world. I have done what is foolish to the world because I wanted to listen to God and not what the world was teaching. I can tell you that none of these things brought me any shame. God only ever encouraged me and never failed me.

REFLECTIONS

1. Has God ever asked you to do something simple? Do you know why He asked you to do it? Have you experienced God's goodness in that situation?

2. What does obedience mean to you?
   What does obedience look like to you?

3. Do you classify yourself as an obedient person?

10

Relationships

Family

"A new commandment I give to you, that you love one another: just as I have loved you, you also are to love one another." (John 13:34, ESV)

It is said that we don't get to choose our family because we are born into it. Some of the most challenging relationships are found within families. There are times when I have been challenged to keep peace with my own parents and siblings. Because God has made each of us different, we often spend much of our day with people whose opinions and perspectives are completely different from our own. It can be challenging to love others through disagreements and arguments.

When we cannot find common ground and we know that we never will because we have vastly different perspectives, let us remember the encouragement of Jesus. Jesus simply reminds us that He loves us and wants us to love each other. There are no conditions to His love. He gave away His life that we might have eternal life – while we were still sinners. The bar He has set is high. If we follow Him and His commands, then we must learn to love even when we don't want to.

I am aware that everyone's family is different and not everyone has loving parents and siblings. If there is control, manipulation or abuse in any form, then you should absolutely walk away or keep boundaries depending upon the situation. But, in such cases, I encourage you to forgive and shake the dust off your feet, so to speak, so that you are not bound by any grudge. Unforgiveness can become a tool for the enemy to use against you. And without forgiveness you can never truly walk in freedom.

Forgiveness shows that we understand God chose to forgive us even while we were sinners. When you forgive someone in your family, it does not necessarily mean immediate reconciliation. This may just sweep problems under the rug. That doesn't do anyone any good. It is imperative to not take forgiveness lightly but to take it to the Lord so that He can help guide you and walk with you in it.

Sometimes He may ask you to reconcile and other times He may not. Sometimes He may ask you to stay in a relationship with healthy boundaries and other times He may ask you to walk away. Traumas, betrayals, abuse and violation of one's boundaries take a long time to heal. Sometimes it is miraculous, other times you may need either pastoral care or therapy. I would urge you to remember that God loves you and you are made in His image and there is no way He wants you to tolerate something that causes you to lose your mental health or physical health. I promise you, forgiving does not mean reconciliation.

The Scriptures ask us to honor our parents. God wants us to be devoted to one another in love and honor others above ourselves (Romans 12:10). Even when we don't feel like it, honoring our family brings us honor and the blessing of a life in which everything works out for our good (Ephesians 6:3). I heard a preacher tell his story one day - his father taught him that he needed to dress up in formal pants and not just a hoodie and sweatpants when he went to church. Initially, he didn't listen to his father. He just didn't want to. Then one day Holy Spirit convicted him - He asked this preacher why he wasn't doing what his father requested. He realized there was no particular reason - he just didn't want to.

He was caught. It was pride that was stopping him from honoring his father's words. Next day he went to the youth group dressed in formal pants and a shirt. Initially, he felt awkward but got used to it. This was a way that Holy Spirit led him to honor his father.

It is such a small, unimportant thing but even in this God wanted the preacher to show his father honor. You see, if we can't honor our earthly parents how are we going to honor our Heavenly Father? How can we bring Him glory when we are so caught up in doing things our own way?

Friendships

"Greater love has no one than this, that someone lay down his life for his friends." (John 15:13, ESV)

Jesus is the ultimate example of a friendship that is God honoring. Before your brain starts racing, yes, even friendships can be God honoring. God can use good friends to bring you closer to Him. One example of such a friendship in the Bible is David and Jonathan. Jonathan helped David every step of the way. He was the son of King Saul, an heir to his kingdom, but he understood his assignment. He knew he was supposed to become the best example of a friend.

If you have friends like Jonathan who are willing to help you in every conceivable way, then you must do everything to keep their company. But if your friends have bad character then it is necessary that you part ways with them. Proverbs say that bad company corrupts good morals. If you surround yourself with failures and procrastinators, then it is more than likely you will follow the same path. The saying,

"Show me your five closest friends, and I will show you your future" begs the questions – who are your friends?

"Blessed is the one who does not walk in step with the wicked or stand in the way that sinners take or sit in the company of mockers." (Psalm 1:1)

Wicked are the ones whose delight is not in the Lord but in the world. In order to be blessed, we need to stay away from those who live in sin. According to Psalm 1, doing so we are called blessed and like fruitful trees planted by the stream of water. The opposite of fruitful is unfruitful. When we are yoked in any way with people who live a lifestyle of sin, we will not be fruitful. It means whatever we do, no matter how much effort and hard work we put in, we won't bear fruit. This sounds like a curse to me. When we are yoked with sinners, we bring the curse of fruitlessness upon ourselves.

God has given us free will. There is life and there is death. Choose life. There is blessing and there is a curse, choose blessing. The choice is ours. So, I encourage you to listen to the guidance of Holy Spirit when choosing friends. Because unlike family, we can choose our friends.

In saying that, I believe there are people who are specifically called evangelize people who live in sin through friendships. But not everyone belongs to that category. For me, I know my friends need to be godly. I have been friends with worldly people and that is not for me. I have been friends with new Christians, and I can mentor them, but friendship with them is not for me. All the fulfilling friendships I have are with people who are mature in Christ, who know the Word and love the Scriptures. I enjoy discussing Jesus and the Scriptures with such people.

Bad company corrupts good morals. This is a story as old as time. God uses friends and peers to get through to us in a way no one else can. You may have friends who are great but have addiction issues or are too worldly, or don't believe in God or a Creator who challenge you and argue with you. Without realizing it, you also start doubting God. These little tricks of the enemy slowly but surely chip away the fear of the Lord. Then you are on the slippery slope to backsliding.

Sometimes the enemy uses our peers to induce insecurities in us. When I was still in school, I had beautiful friends, and I didn't see myself as the pretty one. Naturally, they used to get all the attention and I didn't. They were in relationships at the tender age of fourteen and I was not. This made me feel insecure about not being enough and hating the way I looked. I also had intelligent friends who I compared myself with. Again, I fell short on the cultural scale of intelligence. I was not a teacher's pet nor was I smart enough according to the world. I had issues with myself and so I turned away from God. I had successfully strayed away from all the biblical teaching I had been taught. It took many years, and a great deal of isolation from the rest of the world before I understood God and His goodness for me.

I prefer using wisdom and discernment when choosing friends rather than taking a detour back to God after straying away from His grace and love.

Romantic Relationships
"God is Love." (1 John 4:8)

All the fairy tales for little girls show their need of a man in the form of a savior. So, growing up many little girls dream of their own "prince." It is wired into their minds that their lives are incomplete without a man. As a result, this subconsciously takes root in their minds. This can be dangerous in so many ways. I have seen many women fall for the wrong man in their desperate need to feel complete.

Now, the desire to have companionship and a romantic partner is wired into a woman's DNA. Eve was created for companionship and support. She was created *for* Adam. Adam is commanded to leave his mother and father and cleave to Eve. There is no such command for a woman because she naturally leaves and cleaves, as she was designed to do. Therefore, women sacrifice more for love, dream more for their future partner, and wait more for their partner to change. Your desire to be with a suitable man is natural. But first, God wants us to be closer to Him so He can 'make' us into who we are supposed to be in order for Him to give us someone whom He has for us.

There is no human love in this world that can compare to the love of God. God Himself is love. He is the embodiment of love. In my teenage years, I found myself longing for that kind of love. In the search for it, I got entangled in relationships that didn't glorify God in any way. Those relationships were not true to who I was meant to be or who God wanted me to be. Sometimes, the enemy uses such relationships as a distraction to pull you away from God and godly people.

Dating someone may give you the illusion of completeness. It may even make you feel content for a time. The illusion does eventually fade away though, whether it takes months or years, but it does fade away. Real contentment cannot be obtained without God. Everything will disappear; the only thing that remains is the love of God. As women, we need to change our perspective. Focusing on needing the love of a man will only create a deeper void, because the focus originates from a feeling of lack. Women focus on how they do not have and so therefore don't deserve, the love of a man and settle for something that may just be a distraction to drag them away from their destiny.

Pursuit of God is what brings real joy and fulfillment. In everything we do we seek to please the Lord which keeps us away from anything that may not bring glory to God. God leads us into the right relationship in His time. The standard of which is biblical in every sense. Then it is easy to recognize the right relationship because of our relationship with Jesus and Holy Spirit. So, until God brings the right man into your life, make it a point to reject anything that is ungodly and unbiblical, no matter how attractive it may seem according to the standard of the world. There is wisdom in seeking God first so that He can give you everything you need according to His riches.

"He who finds a wife finds a good thing and obtains favor from the Lord." (Proverbs 18:22, ESV)

In a culture where everything is backwards and women pursue men, the word of God indicates something different. In Proverbs it says that he who finds a wife finds a good thing. A man is the one who pursues a woman. It also states that a prudent wife is from the Lord. So, when a man pursues, God rewards him with a prudent wife. And finding a wife brings him favor. To God, women are the gift and reward. Because of a woman, a man obtains favor.

This is a beautiful thought to me. But the world has contaminated it. Just like in the garden of Eden, the snake is still using his whispers to lead women astray from the beautiful companionship that is shared between a man, a woman and God. Culture has lied to women, making them think that doing everything for a man - living with them, having physical relationships with them and behaving like a wife without marriage, is what sets them free. However, when such a relationship ends it is disastrous for women.

In some cases, women are left with children and children are left without fathers. The enemy hates family. The enemy hates marriage. Anything that becomes a representation of the love of God is hated by the enemy. There is a great need for us to discern the times we are living in, and to know the biblical precedent for marriage and relationships and what is required of us as women.

Men are the head of a family, but women are called the crown. They bring perspective to the head. They bring responsibility to the head and so, any decision that a man makes, he has his crown to be accountable to. Culture tells you it is not good to submit to a man. It means that somehow you are lesser than a man. To me it looks like another lie spurned without any revelation. It is important to understand that a crown is the glory of a man. It brings glory to a man. It brings value to a man.

In relationships, it is important that women know the value God has placed on them. You will not find the true value of women by looking at the world, movies, culture, or fairytales. Look for your value in the Scriptures. Seek the presence of the Lord and ask Him to show you how He sees you. How He sees me and what He has planned for me is completely different to what He has planned for you. Only God can show you what He wants you to be in any relationship, be it as a daughter, sister, wife or friend. Only God can define your true identity and your true value.

When you have a clear idea of how God values you, you will never accept anything less than what God has for you. It will be clear to you when the people around you don't treat you according to your value, and it will be easier for you to walk away from such people and relationships. Why would you, a daughter of a King, accept mistreatment?

All healthy relationships depend upon your perspective - whether you come to them from a position of lack or come to them with an already content heart.

"Do not be unequally yoked with unbelievers. For what partnership does righteousness have with lawlessness? Or what fellowship has light with darkness? (2 Corinthians 6:14, ESV)

When a farmer ploughs a field, two oxen are yoked together. It is imperative to notice that both the oxen need to move at the same pace. When one moves faster than the other, it throws the yoke off balance. The plough will no longer work if it is out of balance. Generally, this is a great metaphor for marriage.

Unequally yoked can also apply to other relationships in life. Even in business partnerships, friendships and other relationships, because the purpose of all relationships is to further the kingdom of God. When they are off-balance for some reason, the field cannot be ploughed - in other words their purpose cannot be fulfilled, and broken hearts inevitably follow. But more so than that, my personal experience is that when I was unequally yoked in a business partnership, the business never took off. I tried to partner with a friend who does not know the Lord but after the launch it never took off. Even the contacts didn't work. The blessing just wasn't there. This business partner of mine is not a wicked or evil person. In fact, she is a good person according to the world. But according to the Bible any person that rejects Jesus is evil. It is as simple as that. And when we walk with the wicked, we cannot expect the blessing of the Lord on the work of our hands. (Psalm 1:1-3, NIV)

So, think about honoring God or at least prioritizing what the Word of God says. not just in romantic relationships but in all the relationships that you may have. There are real consequences to being unequally yoked in relationships, just like there are consequences to everything else. I do wish I had someone speaking these truths into my life when I was younger. It would have saved me a lot of time as well as money.

More discernment is needed as far as marriage is concerned. When two people become one, two legacies become one. With that comes many spiritual battles. Together you plough the field, removing all the weeds and other unwanted plants.

While you wait for someone, you can focus on creating a legacy of your own.

"The name of the Lord is a fortified tower; the righteous run to it and are safe." (Proverbs 18:10)

The only relationship that we can run to safely is a relationship with God. He is the one who not only loved us first but gave Himself for us so that death could not have a hold on us. When we are in right standing with Him, we can run to Him and be safe. The secret place is where we can run and hide. The only relationship that has the power to sustain us, is our relationship with God. Not only that, but it serves as a foundation that all our other relationships can be built on. But first and foremost, we need to be in a relationship with God. There needs to be a longing to be in a conversation with Him. Going to church on Sundays and then expecting God to show up for you while you forget Him for the rest of the week is not a relationship.

I want to encourage you to think in a manner that is Biblical when people in your relationships test you. Think about how God died for them as well. Instead of dwelling on the argument or disagreement, dwell on the fact that Jesus shed His blood for them too. When Peter cut off the ear of a Roman soldier because he came to arrest Jesus, Jesus had a different perspective. He healed the cut-off ear and even reprimanded Peter for using his sword. God's way is different. Jesus was getting ready to do something far greater than Peter could have ever imagined. I am sure the Roman soldier would not have been able to fathom the kindness shown to him. He may have considered the divinity of Christ after all.

Also, if the person you are in a relationship with is a Christian, think about how God will also use the disagreement with you for their own good, just like He will for you. You may not want to show kindness or even talk to them, but it is necessary for your own right standing with the Lord to think in a manner that glorifies God. Christ is in them too. I often think it's my pride that makes me hold a grudge against someone. Somehow, it's just me thinking I am holier and more correct than they are. I have to ask God to show me a different perspective so that I can see the situation from His point of view.

REFLECTIONS

1. How do you glorify God through all your relationships?

2. Think about the challenges you face in all your relationships.
   Write down the struggle and take it to God.
   Ask Him to show you His perspective.
   How does He see that person?
   How does He see your relationship?

3. Is there any relationship in your life where you are unequally yoked?

11

Healing

"But he was pierced for our transgressions, he was crushed for our iniquities; the punishment that brought us peace was on him, and by his wounds we are healed." (Isaiah 53:5, NKJV)

God cares about our wounds. Which is why He bore all of our sickness and sins on Himself at the cross. His doing so made healing available to us. Whether the healing is mental, physical or emotional, it is made available to us through Jesus. The Scripture says that whatever we ask for in His name will be given to us. (John 14:13-17)

But first we need to recognize our need for healing. In reality, it takes a lot to put your pride aside and acknowledge that you may need healing. Emotional and mental wounds are much harder to acknowledge. Some wounds take years to appear on the surface. Being bullied, facing tragedies like losing a loved one, experiencing betrayal and many other things, make us vulnerable to emotional wounds. Scars that are visible are easier to heal.

Growing up we had to face many financial struggles as a family. I don't remember celebrating my birthday. Nothing much happened apart from the cake cutting. I never knew that this was a wound for me. I went to my friends' birthday parties, but I never really thought about the fact that I never had one. Some hurts don't show up in a usual way. God has to bring them up using His creativity. He does it not to hurt us but to heal those areas of our lives so that He can mature our giftings and callings inside of us.

Our thought patterns may reflect hurts we may have received. At the time things may have looked normal to us but as we grow closer to the Lord, He reveals to us our own hearts. Children who grow up in an abusive household or a household with addictions, or a home where curse words are normal and language is never controlled, would think those things are normal until they go out and see other kids in their homes. These examples are extreme, but these things shape our worldview, and this is why Paul asks us to constantly renew our minds - so that our thinking patterns are renewed and come into alignment with the Word.

Because these experiences shape us, it is tough to recognize these patterns. Healing and deliverance are necessary - deliverance from our old self and healing of our hearts.

"Lord my God, I called to you for help, and you healed me." (Psalm 30:2)

Let us rest in the fact that God knows what we need. He knows when we need help and when we need healing. I often think about the story of Elijah where he was hiding from Jezebel because she wanted to kill him. Now, Elijah was not a weak soul. He wasn't just anybody. He was the one who had called down fire from heaven killing four hundred prophets of Baal. But he wasn't in a good place mentally after he received a death threat from Jezebel.

He was in utter despair and his complaint to the Lord was that he was the only one left among God's messengers and now he would most likely be killed by the evil queen too. God met Elijah where he was - he didn't kill the queen or ask him to fight. He simply asked him to rest and eat. Elijah did not understand why he wanted to die but God did. God understood the deep depression that had taken over Elijah. He understood that Elijah was emotionally exhausted and in need of mental rest. God showed up in a way that benefited Elijah the most. He wasn't in a fire or great wind. He showed up in a whisper. A sweet and gentle voice.

God shows up for us in a way He knows we need Him most. Elijah needed to see the Lord as a gentle God who whispers with love. He needed to hear His healing voice. Let me encourage you to bare your heart to the Lord. Speak to Him all about your cares and worries. He will hear you, reveal Himself to you and heal you.

"Have mercy on me, Lord, I am faint; heal me, Lord, for my bones are in agony." (Psalm 6:2)

King David knew how to open his heart to the Lord so that he could heal him completely. There were things David didn't even know he had inside of him that needed purging and healing. Which is why he asked God to search his heart and heal it of any iniquities. If God could do it for David, He is more than capable of doing it for us too.

"He heals the broken-hearted and binds up their wounds." (Psalm 147:3)

God is close to the brokenhearted. He cares for our wounds, applies His healing balm and binds our wounds for us. He has healed me of things I didn't know I was holding on to. My wounds manifested as bitterness, anger and unforgiveness. It took God some time to show me the root of this behavior. It was a broken heart and a wound that needed binding. Little by little He did work on and me and He will do it for you too.

If our heart is not healed, out of it flows the issues of life. Your vision and your perspective become tainted. Moreover, as I got stuck in a cycle of bitterness and anger, I was in danger of never being able to move forward. An unhealed heart has a way of holding us in a prison of the past. We need to acknowledge our broken heart so that it can be healed and we can be set free from the past.

My first born was born by cesarean section, so naturally I have a scar. When I was pregnant with my second born and went for a routine checkup with a midwife, she told me something that has stayed with me ever since. She saw my scar and said, "Oh you have a thick scar." I had never been conscious of it before. The moment she said it, my brain went into overdrive thinking that there was something wrong with my scar. But she immediately said, "Don't worry, everyone heals differently." When I left the appointment, I realized God had spoken to me through that simple statement. I had been in a difficult place emotionally and was thinking that something was wrong with me as I was not getting healed quickly enough. But the Lord spoke through that midwife, "Everyone heals differently."

Scars for each person may look different and so will our healing journeys. God's work will look different in each of our lives. The time it takes for you to obtain complete healing and deliverance may also look different. Nevertheless, the Holy Spirit works behind the scenes to bring about God's complete healing.

"People brought to them all who were ill...... and he healed them." (Matthew 4:24)

Jesus healed all who were brought to him. Those who went to Him willingly and in faith, and those who were brought to Him in faith, were all healed. This scripture brings me so much hope. It assures us that we are covered in grace because of Jesus and He does what we ask of Him in His name. He heals us when we go to Him. In fact, we should bring others to Him in prayer as well.

If someone around us needs healing, whether in their bodies, minds or hearts, we can bring them to Jesus in prayer. The Lord heals all sickness, according to Psalm 103:3.

REFLECTIONS

1. Has God revealed to you an area where you may need healing? Has reading this chapter helped you recognise any hidden wound?

2. Have you been healed of any known or unknown wound or trauma with the help of the Holy Spirit?

3. Have you ever prayed for someone who got healed?
   On the contrary, have you prayed for someone
   who did not get healed?
   What are your thoughts on both of these situations?

12

Righteousness Of Christ

"God made him who had no sin to be sin for us, so that in him we might become righteousness of God." (2 Corinthians 5:21)

There was a great exchange that took place on the cross. Because Jesus was holy and righteous, He offered it to us so that we may become righteous. Our sins were placed on Him so that we may boldly go before the throne of the Father through the blood of Jesus. When we believe in Jesus and He cleanses us with His blood, we become righteous through grace in the sight of the Father.

We are asked to seek and pursue righteousness so that we may glorify God through our lives. What does pursuing righteousness really mean? It means that we have free will to choose momentary pleasure under the influence of our flesh, or we can learn the art of training our flesh once we realize that there is a standard of holiness and that is Jesus Christ.

One night I was sitting alone on the edge of my bed trying to put my newborn daughter to sleep. There were things conspiring in my life at that time which had not only left me heartbroken but also with hope deferred. I was talking to the Lord about my woes. And then suddenly

He started speaking. My question to Him was this: there are people who sin against God and against the people of God. These individuals are often well-meaning Christians who somehow fall into the enemy's trap along the way — but how does that happen? I would never intentionally do something to hurt someone, so why does it seem easier for some people to do so? God had a clear answer, "Because their standard of righteousness comes from within themselves and not from God." There are two types of people. Firstly, there are 'God people,' whose standard of righteousness comes from God. There is this constant yearning inside of them to be holy even as the Lord is holy. Of course, their conviction comes from the Holy Spirit; He is the one who helps us along the journey. When God is our standard, it becomes impossible to let compromise enter that space. When the righteousness of Jesus Christ lives within us, we never want to trade it off for a momentary compromise.

Secondly, there are the 'good people.' Good people believe in doing good. Even though they are Christians and are born again, their standard of goodness comes from their own moral compass. Righteousness comes from within themselves. Such holiness is easily compromised. We can compromise our standards little by little just enough to adjust our standard of holiness to serve us, and in doing so we completely stray from the righteous One Himself. Therefore, anything becomes permissible.

Choosing to be in right standing with the Lord rather than being justified by the culture around us is what righteousness looks like. To the world, the standards of God look foolish and of no value. To the people around you, a little gossip might be okay. But when the Holy Spirit lives inside of you, you already feel convicted and disgusted even with such things going on around you, let alone when you do them yourself.

The righteousness of Christ looks like choosing to refrain from watching a certain movie or a show, choosing to stay away from gossip and making clear boundaries with friends that may lead you astray. As we live in the Word, we become aware of how holy God is and how He wants us to be holy. This knowledge creates an innate desire to imitate Christ in every aspect of our lives. When we sacrifice our flesh and take on Christ, we become a sweet aroma of Christ to the Father. But we become a stench to this world.

People have a tendency to dislike someone when their mere presence makes them aware of their own shortcomings. Just by telling them that you do not participate in gossip or in office politics, they are reminded of when they indulged in such things, and as a result they dislike you. You become like a stench to them. Living in right standing with God will offend worldly people. But I'd rather offend people than follow in their footsteps. If you are led by Holy Spirit, it is more than likely that you will offend someone.

This will also help you recognize God ordained relationships in your life. The righteousness of Christ will attract the same type of friends and will sift out all the ungodly and unequally yoked relationships.

"...the righteous are as bold as a lion." (Proverbs 28:1)

Living one's life in a holy fashion means living in complete surrender to God's voice and the Scriptures. The world challenges young women with the notion of liberty and independence. To the world freedom means dressing provocatively, having multiple sexual relationships before marriage, glorifying abortion and despising the covenant relationship of marriage. While living in righteousness means living in modesty and purity, honoring life and the covenant relationship of marriage. When you honor what God honors, you go against the grain of today's culture.

The word independence is thrown around loosely to encourage women to live an unrighteous life. But the reality is the more you live like the world, satisfying all your ungodly whims and desires, the more you are trapped in the bondage of sin. And the more access you give to the enemy. True freedom is in surrendering your life to Christ. True freedom brings boldness. When your standard of righteousness comes from God, you can come boldly to the throne of the Father. And according to James 5:16, the prayer of the righteous is powerful and effective. There arises a boldness within you when you are free from condemnation.

The Pharisees and Sadducees kept the law to a T, and then some. They performed every ritual and followed every command given in the Torah - literally. They tried to be physically righteous in every possible way. But Jesus gives a new command in Matthew 5. He says that even if you are angry with your brother, you have already murdered him in your heart. If you look at a woman with lust, you have already committed adultery. Jesus is affirming the concept in Proverbs 4:23 - that out of our hearts flow the issues of life.

Righteousness is a heart issue. Righteousness cannot be defined by 'outside-in,' but it is defined by 'inside-out.' First the heart is brought into alignment with God's standard of righteousness and then our actions will follow.

I encourage you to go against the grain and be everything that the world needs you to not be. Surrender yourself at the feet of the cross. Bring the living sacrifice of your flesh and its desires to the altar. Be modest and pure and full of integrity. Trade your sin for the righteousness of Christ.

REFLECTIONS

1. Do you consider yourself a "God people" or a "good people."

2. Have you ever compromised on the standard of the righteousness of God?
   What were the consequences?
   Would you do anything differently now?

13

Biblical Femininity

"Charm is deceptive, and beauty is fleeting; but a woman who fears the LORD is to be praised." (Proverbs 31:30)

There are many teachers and preachers who talk about biblical femininity. There are many podcasts highlighting the importance of walking in femininity as defined by the scriptures. There may be misconceptions that femininity is submissive, and woman needs to be under a man. This notion has fooled an entire generation of women who now subconsciously accept the idea of what a strong and independent woman is, as defined by culture - a woman who is harsh and climbs the ladder of her career is praised; a woman who keeps on dating and never marrying is applauded for not settling; a woman who gives her body to any and everyone is praised as open minded and sexually expressive (whatever that means). Women who are attracted by such 'femininity' do not understand the value that God has placed on women. To God, women are valuable.

Genesis 5:2 states that God created man and woman in His image. Women are made in the image of God. Maybe God's nature is so all encompassing that neither only a man nor only a woman could carry the fullness of His nature. Maybe that is the reason He divided His nature and His image into male and female. Whatever the reason, women are made in His image. Scripture is clear about that. There is no argument about it.

When I read Proverbs 31 for the first time, I found a strong and independent woman. A woman who takes care of her husband and her children but is also a woman who negotiates a deal and buys real estate. She is an investor who invests the money made from her deal. She is a businesswoman who knits bed coverings and makes linen garments. Moreover, she also takes care of her servant girls by providing food for them. She is generous to the poor. Her worth is more than rubies. Her husband is blessed by her, and her children call her blessed. Now, this is a strong woman. The passage then goes on to praise her for her wisdom. This type of wisdom comes only from God.

This is what biblical femininity is all about. It's not just charm or a half-cooked idea of independence. It shows grit, wisdom, hard work and strong character. I do understand that not everyone will possess all of these qualities. The passage then makes it clear that a woman who fears the Lord is to be praised.

The fear of the Lord is the test for true character. You will always follow Jesus and be more like Christ when you have the fear of the Lord. Because the fear of the Lord is where wisdom begins. A woman can have great values and principles but when the fear of the Lord is missing, it becomes easier to compromise on morality.

I used to think that in order to become this woman, I needed to do all the things that the Proverbs 31 woman does. But God is not asking us to do everything the woman in this chapter is doing. The key quality that God has placed inside of her is what is valuable. And that key quality is wisdom. And not just any wisdom but, Godly wisdom.

"Wives, submit to your own husbands as you do to the Lord." (Ephesians 5:22)

I have seen this verse being used incorrectly and out of context many times. People love to say that it says a woman must be submissive to a man. But the passage is exclusively about the covenant relationship of marriage, where a wife is asked to submit to her husband. The word is 'submit' not 'submissive.' The word 'submissive' portrays a person who is passively obedient. It colors the marital relationship in a negative light. The word 'submit' means to yield. And yielding happens with careful consideration, and willingly.

Wives are to submit to their husbands like the Church submits to Christ. And husbands are to love their wives as Christ loves the church. We fail to recognize while arguing about the role of a woman in marriage, that husbands are held to the standard of Christ. Christ loved the church by giving His life for her. The standard is far higher. Husbands are asked to show this sacrificial love.

There is a saying in the secular world, that if a man is the head of the household, then the woman is the neck. It implies that women manipulate men into making decisions, thereby creating an illusion that the men are the ones leading their home and families. But a biblical woman is different. According to Proverbs 12:4, "A virtuous woman is her husband's crown." A good woman is her husband's pride and honor. Woman are held to a high standard in the Bible, while the world only gives an illusion of a high standard for women.

Being generous, gentle, humble, kind, wise and yielding is what biblical femininity is about. It's also about being hardworking, successful in the marketplace and contributing to society as well as the home. A woman who is worth more than rubies is a woman who loves and cares deeply. Biblical womanhood is not just about being married and having children. Rather it is about glorifying God in everything we do while at the same time honoring our design as a woman.

If we decide to work, let it be done in a way that brings glory to God. It means giving your excellent efforts even when nobody is watching. Choosing integrity over momentary rest and pleasure. Joseph could have given in to the desires of Potipher's wife because no one was watching. But he chose to honor God even in that situation. The little girl who was brought as a slave into Naman's house, chose to become the reason Naman was free from debilitating leprosy.

Biblical women are strong like Deborah without whom Barak didn't go to war and also soft and meek like Jael, offering warm milk and rest to Sisera before driving a tent peg into his temple. These qualities do matter, but ultimately the blueprint to biblical femininity is a woman who fears the Lord. Biblical womanhood is defined by the reverential fear of the Lord because that is what brings everything else into order.

REFLECTIONS

1. How do you define femininity? Is your idea of femininity similar or different to biblical femininity?

2. Has your opinion about biblical womanhood changed or remained the same after reading this chapter?

14

Daily Declarations:

I like to declare these things over myself first thing in the morning. You can add your own scriptures and declare them each morning.

> I AM FEARFULLY AND WONDERFULLY MADE
> (Psalm 139:14)
> I AM MADE IN THE IMAGE OF GOD
> (Genesis 1:2)
> I AM FAVORED BY MAN AND GOD ALIKE
> (Luke 2:52)
> I AM BLESSED IN MY COMING AND GOING
> (Deuteronomy 28:6)
> I AM THE HEAD AND NOT THE TAIL. I AM ABOVE
> AND NOT BENEATH (Deuteronomy 28:13)
> I AM VICTORIOUS
> (Romans 8:37)
> BY THE STRIPES OF JESUS I AM HEALED
> (Isaiah 53:5)
> I AM ADVANCING FROM GLORY TO GLORY
> (2 Corinthians 3:18)

www.ingramcontent.com/pod-product-compliance
Lightning Source LLC
Chambersburg PA
CBHW061729070526
44583CB00024B/3066